D1527373

$5 FOR A CAT HEAD

True stories of animal welfare,
with hands-on tips for helping animals

Linda Chitwood

Director, The Homeless Animals Relief Project

Dedication

THIS BOOK IS dedicated to the memory of Tommy K. Chitwood, without whom our progress against animal suffering would never have been possible. We also remember the other animal welfare advocates who've gone ahead of us on the journey home, but whose compassion and respect for animals helped, supported, inspired, and motivated us:

Annie Lee Roberts

Dallas Pratt

Paul Jolly

Muriel Slodden

Our sincere thanks and gratitude also to The Summerlee Foundation and Marian's Dream for grant support that has made this book possible, and for their mentorship of The Homeless Animals Relief Project (HARP) since inception. Because of their generosity, 100% of the profits from this book will belong to the animals and will provide for their spay/neuter surgeries.

It would be impossible to list every donor and every organization that has supported our battle against animal overpopulation and animal suffering in rural Mississippi. But some of the others who bolstered and nurtured HARP and made this progress possible include:

The PETCO Foundation
The Two Mauds Foundation
Esther Mechler, Founder, FixByFive campaign and SPAY/USA.

Melanie Anderson, Animal Protection Program Director, The Summerlee Foundation

Alex Brinkley, JD

The Petsmart Foundation

MS Board of Animal Health

Our incredible, amazing veterinarians and our CPA, who've all given so selflessly of their skills

Our selfless volunteers and the veterinary students who gave of their time to help less fortunate animals

The donors who've written checks, some big and some small. Every bit helps.

You can help too by donating:

Homeless Animals Relief Project

POB 371

Senatobia MS 38668

There were four people named Everybody, Somebody, Anybody, and Nobody. There was an important job to be done and Everybody was sure that Somebody would do it. Anybody could have done it, but Nobody did it. Somebody got angry about that because it was Everybody's job. Everybody thought that Anybody could do it, but Nobody realized that Everybody wouldn't do it. It ended up that Everybody blamed Somebody when Nobody did what Anybody could have done.

— Author unknown

Text and photos © 2019 Linda Chitwood
& The Homeless Animals Relief Project

P. O. Box 371
Senatobia MS 38668

Print ISBN: 978-1-54399-194-9
eBook ISBN: 978-1-54399-195-6

CONTENTS

Foreword

IN 1990, U.S. shelters were euthanizing twelve million cats and dogs—each year. I remember this because it was 'a million a month.' Something had to be done.

Motivated by what I saw in my backyard of Bridgeport, Connecticut, I asked my veterinarian, Dr. Arnold Brown, if he would spay or neuter cats and dogs that our program referred to him at a special discount. He said yes. He was the first. Clearly the problems in Bridgeport were the same all over the country, and so the SPAY/USA program was started. Within three years, we had affordable programs and clinics in all fifty states. It is an indication of how great the need was that in May, 1993 an article about the program in *Cat Fancy* magazine resulted in 23,000 calls to our hotline, 1-800-248-SPAY.

The two most gratifying aspects of running this program were 1), knowing that tens of thousands of people each year were able to gain access to affordable, accessible cat/dog spay/neuter services locally and 2), hearing from grassroots people all around the country who were making a difference in their own cities and towns.

I well remember Linda Chitwood's first call to our hotline. It was in the late 1990s, and she inquired about a problem with numerous stray cats in a mobile home park near her hometown.

It was clear as we spoke that she knew how to go about solving this daunting problem and so I listened, thinking that if someone else called with a similar issue, her thoughts would be very helpful. I remember thinking this knowledge needs to be shared. She knew about the basic, key need to stop the cycle of unwanted litters. She understood about the kindest and most effective ways to convince people to help. She knew how to find out who is in control and who can give permission and assistance. She knew what actions would lead to a dead end.

Unbeknownst to me, Melanie Anderson of the Summerlee Foundation was also thinking that Linda should write a book. It would be years before Linda would have the time and energy to put it together, but she has done it!

This book is the perfect gift for the young friend, neighbor or relation who wants to help animals but does not know where to start. Or for the retiree who now has time to do what he or she dearly wants to do. Or for anyone who wants to make a real difference in real life.

Years ago, volunteers made huge differences in their communities, but our culture has now drifted off to a place where people just send a check and hope the problems go away. They do not go away. It is time to get back to direct action, one-on-one help, and compassionate caring. Linda Chitwood shows us how with specific tips, do's and don'ts, all woven into very compelling true stories that play out in trailer parks, alleyways and parking lots. This book made me smile, it made me cry, and it made me hopeful.

A very moving, very powerful book, much needed at this time.

—Esther Mechler, Founder, FixByFive campaign and SPAY/USA.

October, 2019

Preface

THE HOMELESS ANIMALS Relief Project (HARP) is an independent, tiny grass roots effort I launched in 1996 and formerly incorporated as a 501(c)3 nonprofit charity in 2000. Our mission is to provide free or very low cost spay/neuter surgery (pet birth control surgery) and basic medical care to animals living with the poor, and to feral cats.

Once I plunged into the spay/neuter movement, acquaintances would ask why I got involved, and how we accomplish our mission. With the help and support of dedicated animal welfare advocates, our organization has put thousands of dogs and cats on the surgery table for spay or neuter, all on a shoe-string budget. Some assume that I am a veterinarian (I'm not), and many believe we must be affiliated with or supported by the major national animal welfare groups in America (we're not). Everyone unanimously assumes we are a rescue group. We are not. Our focus is on *stopping* the flow of homeless animals, animals who will be euthanized or killed because there are no homes with vacancies. While you will read stories of rescued animals in this book, we remained focused on providing spay/neuter surgery because that STOPS the production of puppies and kittens for whom there will be no homes. It ends, right then with that surgery, the legions of homeless pets who must be rescued from hunger, hurt, and homelessness, or more likely, be euthanized as excess.

Because of the mission, we receive calls and emails from other advocates, asking for advice on how to get money to cover the surgeries, how to reach low-income people to let them know of the services, how to start a spay/neuter surgery program. Much of this information is instantly available on the internet, but it may be buried in a daunting volume of results. Hands-on advice for targeting animals living with the poor may be limited. Targeting the poor is critical though, as the majority of pet overpopulation will be found in low-income areas. After the encouragement of mentors, I've written this book as a primer on how you can begin to stop animal suffering and overpopulation in your community, even just one animal at a time, through spay/neuter surgery. No multimillion-dollar budget, no two million-dollar surgical facility, no army of volunteers, no full-time commitment required. Maybe you'll build all that one day, and please do! But start small, start manageable.

This book proves you don't need a big budget or big blocks of time to help animals. You don't have to commit your life to it if you don't want to or can't. Your top priority though is: Stop the flood of homeless animals with spay/neuter surgery. If you love animals, begin by helping one. Think one cat fixed isn't much? Consider cat reproduction: Two to three litters per year, with females coming into heat as early as 14 weeks; male cats fathering dozens or more kittens per year. Fact: Fixing one cat saves thousands. And it saves the thousands of dollars needed to manage and control the homeless offspring if the cat isn't fixed. Focusing on spay/neuter surgery, our limited number of volunteers have improved the health and welfare of thousands of animals, dramatically dropped animal overpopulation in our area, and enhanced our community's health through vaccinated, sterile animals. All with mostly volunteer labor and a tiny budget.

Although this book relates our volunteers' efforts to get pets fixed, the most important lives described in $5 For a Cat Head are the incredible, fabulous, glorious, and spunky creatures the book is all about, these precious creatures for whom we all toil. Dogs and cats down on their luck, but still unlimited in their love for us. Radiating their forgiving, tender, adorable, and mysterious personalities, their enchanting beauty and proud bearing remain a feast for our eyes. They are the reason we do what we do. Because these cats and dogs cannot describe their lives for you, cannot speak their histories, cannot tell you of their pain or joy, hunger or happiness, I've tried to capture that for you in each tale. I am inadequate in that endeavor. But still, please draw inspiration from these animals' lives, and intervene to help the less fortunate cats and dogs found in your community.

$5 For a Cat Head proves you can make a difference, one animal at a time. I've tried to present the basics here of what you need to know to make a difference in one animal's life today. We need those younger and stronger than us to take up the helm and fight to fix animals who otherwise might never get to see a veterinarian in their lives. For the sake of these less fortunate animals, please take the challenge.

$5 For A Cat Head

I REALIZED I'D lived a cushy and innocent life, at least in regard to pet welfare, when I moved to rural Mississippi from Memphis in 1996. Like most urban cities, Memphis has a local animal shelter, animal control officers, and nonprofit animal rescues. Make a phone call and someone else will come pick up that stray cat, drive the injured dog to a vet, or retrieve the unwanted kittens. It didn't always end happily, but at least I never had to dodge a cat trap thrown at me by a drunk, or pluck a cat testicle off my sleeve.

Yet in this new small community, unwanted and discarded pets littered the roads like living trash. Suffering dogs and cats and puppies and kittens, along with cruel practices to control overpopulation and unwanted pet behaviors, seemed almost the norm, not the exception. But I also discovered compassionate, caring, concerned people who loved their pets and wanted to care for them properly, people who beamed with pride as they became the first person on their block to have a cat who'd been fixed and vaccinated, people who would skip their own prescription medicine to be able to feed their dog, people who divvied up what little food they had to share with the elfin stray perched on the sagging stoop of their trailer, and people who would whoop and weep for joy when handed a bag of pet food.

Animal welfare services were pretty much nonexistent here in 1996. With no animal shelters and only two veterinary clinics in the entire county (none in surrounding counties), there were then, and even today, limited choices for less fortunate animals. For low-income people and the poor, spay/neuter surgery to sterilize or "fix" a pet is unheard of. Even for the well-educated and well-off, pet spay/neuter surgery isn't often utilized or is reserved for the females.

Spay/neuter surgery, or animal birth control surgery, must form the foundation of any dog and cat welfare program. Spay/neuter surgery sterilizes the pet so he or she can no longer reproduce. In America it's commonly referred to as "fixing," "altering," or sterilizing a pet. Spay/neuter surgery slashes the need for pet rescue, reduces the killing of unwanted pets, prevents the transmission of disease, improves pet behavior, and enriches pet health. While we've made impressive progress, we are still sadly killing extreme numbers—millions every year—of unwanted pets, especially cats in America. That number has been dropping in past years though, because the simple focus on spay or neuter surgery effects big change.

Realizing that the poor in my community lacked access to affordable and lifesaving spay or neuter surgery for their pets, I began in 1996 by getting cats and dogs spayed, neutered, or "fixed," as most call it, a few at a time. As a nurse anesthetist working in surgery departments, I had access to discarded unused surgical supplies. I bartered that with an energetic young veterinarian in a nearby city, securing his commitment to trade the supplies for a no-cost spay or neuter surgery to a pet living with an indigent owner. To find qualified candidates, I placed an ad in the local weekly paper. The first respondents lived in trailer parks in neighboring counties, and I sent five dogs and seven cats to this vet for surgery over the next two months.

Then a horrified owner of one of those cats called, reporting that the manager of her trailer park was offering the children $5 for the head of every cat they brought to him. "He was kidding, right?" I asked, stunned.

"No, he was not. The children are very busy right now searching for cats," explained the caller.

I called the manager, and to my surprise the grump didn't deny throwing down that challenge to the children. "They knew I was kidding," he claimed.

Teaching cruelty to animals to children as a real or laughing matter is never acceptable and in fact is unethical and immoral, I exclaimed. He retorted that I should mind my own business and he hung up.

Follow the money. It only took a little research to uncover the owner of that trailer park, a prominent family in nearby Memphis, Tennessee. Certain they didn't want their name mentioned in connection with this type of cruelty; I informed this owner of the manager's comments. An hour later the manager was unemployed. The landlord agreed that I could bring in a team to fix the pets currently living in the 32-unit trailer park in this county, which has a staggering unemployment rate linked inevitably to the equally staggering poverty levels. Of course, to fix pets you need vets. I made calls, begged, and pleaded, and on a crisp clear October morning in 1997, a group of five volunteers and three veterinarians descended upon the trailer court. Working in a vacant trailer, we left that afternoon with 36 dogs and cats sterilized and vaccinated. The cost twenty-plus years ago? $300, because everyone was a volunteer, the workspace was donated, and I already had some surgical supplies we could use. That money came from a national spay/neuter organization that took a chance on helping us, a blessing that got us to where we are today.

After that the poor, the elderly, the disabled, and the less fortunate called for help getting their pets fixed. We set up temporary one or two-day pop up spay/neuter surgery clinics in donated buildings; we solicited donations to cover the costs of the animals' care. In 2000 we incorporated as the Homeless Animals Relief Project, and later received 501(c)3 status as a nonprofit organization. At these spay days we would typically sterilize 50 to 100 or more cats and dogs. Today we continue to provide free or very low cost spay/neuter surgery to pets, mostly cats, living with the poor in this area. Still largely an afterthought in some shelters and often ignored by rescues, humane societies, and big donors, cats are proliferating faster than homes become available for them.

If you picked up this book, you probably love animals and have a dog or cat or two or three already. You survey sad ads and disturbing photos of suffering dogs or cats and muse, "I would take them all if I could." Then you feel hopeless because you can't. There are solutions though. And there is hope too. You will find it in this book.

Through the following tales of animals we encountered at the Homeless Animals Relief Project, I hope to inspire you to improve pet welfare in your community by focusing first on getting pets fixed, which means providing or supporting affordable or even free spay/neuter surgery. In $5 For A Cat Head you will:

Read true stories of dogs and cats encountered in 23 years of animal welfare work.

Realize why spay/neuter surgery should be your first priority when promoting pet welfare.

Understand some of the realities low-income pet owners face when trying to care for their pets.

Consider the issues involved in getting dogs off chains.

Explore feral cat concerns.

Learn steps you can take to encourage feline spay/neuter surgery at an early age.

Discover ways you can help others get their pets fixed.

Recognize your responsibilities when offering homeless pets for adoption.

Review some of the reasons people do not properly care for their pets.

Determine potential interventions with injured animals.

Discern the best organizations to which you can donate your money or time.

Find inspiration to improve pet welfare in your community.

Gain perspective on the catchphrase 'no-kill'.

All of the stories here are true. Some names, locations, or details have been changed to protect privacy, but this is fact, not fiction. Each tale ends with the lessons I learned; please use the recounting of any fumbles and successes to carve your own path and dodge my errors. At the end of this book you will find a summary list of hands-on how to tips for helping cats and dogs in your community.

After discussions with mentors about whether or not to include painful and sad stories in this book, we unanimously agreed that both gratifying happy stories and the distressing heartrending tales must be presented, for that is the stark reality of working to improve animal welfare. If you want to help pets in your community, you must confront their suffering to do it. In this book you will read of some sad and disturbing events. I hope the facts presented and the solutions or lessons learned still spur you to intervene for animals in distress who cannot speak for themselves. You will learn about turning some bad situations into happy ones, or at least a better one. This is the sole and only purpose for including any mention of animal suffering or cruelty here. I can't imagine I would have been so directly rocketed into animal welfare advocacy if it had not been for that manager's outrageous and evil offer of cash for a cat head. I probably wouldn't be as involved with feral cats had it not been for hearing of a horrible cruelty stopped by another woman, an advocate who intervened on the cats' behalf. Harness the hurt you feel for these creatures and transform it into advocacy for them.

Also remember you'll read here of the things that worked—or didn't—in the communities of our Southern state, Mississippi. Not everything described or suggested might apply to the situation you face, nor will the way it was handled feel right for you in every case. In fact, it could seem just wrong, especially if you weren't there. But we all toil under a kaleidoscope of circumstances, none of which are ever identical. With longer daylight hours and warmer weather, the Southern states generally face greater pet overpopulation issues than cooler, darker Northern climates. We've also not been as laser-focused on surgical sterilization to reduce pet overpopulation as more progressive and wealthier states have been. You've no doubt seen or heard of homeless pets from the Southern USA being transported to the Northern regions, where pet overpopulation has been reduced. And of course, you don't often find the famous donors, fancy galas, and multimillion-dollar humane organizations in the rural South.

Acknowledging that how we tackled a challenging circumstance here may be different from the approach another advocate might take, please know that both directions might be fruitful and just. I hope you will grasp that painful predicaments and onerous decisions are reflected in these tales. Decisions had to be made. Some in encounters where there was neither a good nor even a right choice. You may not agree with the conclusions drawn or the actions taken. But please know no intervention was undertaken lightly or quickly or without facts and compassion. The best decision we could reach, for what was at stake at that time and within the resources we had available, is what we did. Many of these decisions were troublesome. This is life though, even absent animal welfare issues.

While bearing in mind our regional differences and perhaps varied perspectives, I hope this book will spark a civil and respectful but lively conversation among all of us who love these precious marvelous creatures we call pets. Let this be the beginning of a discussion between you and your friends or neighbors, your coworkers, your family, your community leaders, your elected officials, and veterinary professionals. Discuss the role of sterilization through spay/neuter surgery in reducing pet overpopulation and suffering, and strategize on how to make life-saving spay/neuter surgery available now to anyone who has a pet in your community. Fixing pets early, especially cats before they are five months old, is the sustainable, cost-effective, and humane solution to animal overpopulation and suffering. Rather than daily reacting to unwanted litters and homeless pets by warehousing and euthanizing, a focus on fixing pets propels us to a proactive, positive, hope-filled compassionate animal welfare framework. Next, put your ideas to work in your community for our amazing, mysterious companions from the Animal Kingdom.

CHAPTER 1

Ranger

We have a kitten down

"THIS IS RANGER Charlie Smith at the Park, we have a kitten down, we have a kitten down, we need assistance immediately!"

"I beg your pardon?" I asked, lifting the receiver off my ear because he was shouting so loud. A kitten down?

"We need help immediately! We have a kitten down! We have a kitten down! Hit by car! We need help ma'am!"

"A kitten who's been hit by a car? You need to get it to a vet," I replied. With this recreation area's permission, we'd sterilized a feral cat colony at the public nature area.

"Ma'am, we need help immediately! He's down! I'm not even sure he's breathing!" I heard a choking sound that seemed to be a shuttered sob.

"Okay, will you drive the kitten to the vet?" I repeated, realizing finally he was quite serious about a kitten down.

"We need help here now! We can't leave our posts to drive him! We don't know what to do! Oh no, please, please, please, hurry, hurry, I think he's going to die!" I heard raw pain in his voice.

"Okay, okay, I'll see what I can do," I said, and disconnected so I could call the volunteer I knew to be in the area. A nurse, she works long hours far from her home, but she makes time to help others' animals. Volunteering at our spay/neuter surgery clinic the day before, she was returning some of those pets to their owners. I called her, relieved to hear her say she'd swing by and see what was happening.

Upon arrival, here's what she witnessed: A tiny orange kitten lying in the road, while Park Rangers, emergency lights spinning and flashing on their vehicles, blocked the road on both sides of the kitten. Two Rangers waved traffic past the crash site, and cars gently eased by on the road shoulder, rubber-necking drivers straining to see what the problem was. We have a kitten down!

As the volunteer pulled up, one Ranger stooped and tentatively scooped up the kitten, an orange tabby short-hair male about six-weeks-old. The kitten seemed to be regaining consciousness. Taking the creature from him, the volunteer saw no obvious wounds. With a quick 'thanks,' she drove him to our vet, where the kitten was found to have only a concussion, from which he recovered promptly. Named Ranger after these gentlemen who saved him, he was placed into a loving home after being neutered and vaccinated.

Ranger with the Ranger

The lesson? Sometimes animals are just stunned by a blow and can completely recover if they can be protected until the return of consciousness. And it's heartening to know that others care, especially if you model that behavior so their concern can surface too. Let children see your compassion and kindness to animals in action. Admit it's not "just a cat" to you, it is a living sentient being who feels pain, suffers hunger, thirst, and loneliness, and bonds with his or her companions. There are people who want to help and they will, given the opportunity. Show them it's okay to care that there is a precious little kitten down.

Cats litter up to three times a year. Female kittens can cycle into heat at 14 weeks of age and deliver their first litter around 22 weeks of age before they are actually even adults themselves. Spay/neuter surgery stops that; one cat or dog fixed saves thousands of lives over the coming years. Spay/neuter surgery is the fundamental edict to end animal suffering. A campaign led by national spay/neuter surgery advocate Esther Mechler aims to get all cats fixed by the age of five months, before their first heat. If all American cats were fixed by five, we could eliminate the killing of homeless cats in shelters! Please go to fixbyfive.org to learn more. The exponential reproduction of cats not fixed by age five months leaves America with significant pet overpopulation. Fixing a pet stops that cycle. Because male pets can father dozens of pups or kittens a year, it's vital that we get them in for neutering too. Spaying females before their first heat cycle may reduce or eliminate the risk of breast cancer. Multiple litters can shorten a female pet's life. Spay/neuter surgery is not only the solution to animal overpopulation, but it also benefits a pet over their lifetime through improved health.

CHAPTER 2

Elliott

Burn ban

SADDENED TO SEE a dog baking on the red gravel on the roadside as I returned home late one steamy August afternoon, I assumed he'd been hit by a car. But he lifted his head for just a moment as I drew closer. I pulled off the road and approached him. A male pit bull-type mix, short-hair, mostly white with a brown spot covering half his face, he had gorgeous green-brown eyes and was about twenty pounds of bone and not much else. He didn't lift his head again or move as I spoke to him, but he did thump his tail twice. In breathtakingly horrid condition, this pitiful creature consisted of little more than a skeleton, a beating heart, burnt skin, and a pendulous wormy belly. Mange covered parts of his body, but his trunk mainly consisted of raw, flame red, oozing, peeling, and inflamed tissue. I ran my hands down each of his extremities. No obvious fractures. He didn't respond except to lift his tail again, puffing dusty red clay into the fading sunlight. I encouraged him to stand, but he didn't even open his eyes this time. From the back of my car I pulled two surgical cover gowns. I carry them because they're great for draping over traps with frightened cats, and they spread out nicely to protect the car, which is what I used one of them for this day. Pulling the other over my clothes, I donned a pair of disposable latex gloves, and stooped to lift the dog. No resistance. I laid the animal in the back of my car and drove for home, my mind racing. What could have happened to him? Bypassing the house and pulling up at the barn, I lifted the limp, flaccid bundle from the car. I carried him to a horse stall. Settling him down onto the shavings, I stood shaking my head in astonishment at what really just looked like the skeletal remains of a dog, while my equally stunned spouse went to get him food and water.

Elliott one hour after he was found

Lying motionless, the dog made no attempt to stand. It was quite late to call the veterinarian for routine euthanasia, so I hoped he would eat. Maybe tonight would be this dog's first chance to rest in safety and without hunger or thirst. We placed the food in front of him. Rolling in slow motion onto his breastbone, the dog ate lying down, gulping the kibble with gusto, and then he lapped up the whole bowl of water. I stroked his head and neck, which did have a hair coat, and he fell back onto his side and slept. The next morning, he wolfed down his breakfast again while reclining. When I returned home after work and slid open the stall door that evening, he was sitting. That tail was wagging with some energy now. He opened his mouth and grinned at me, silky green eyes sparkling from a ring of brown around the irises. Hope building, I thought he might just survive.

Elliott two days after he was found

By the following morning the now cheerful dog stood, wagged his tail, and hopped into the car for a trip to the vet. But given the dog's disturbing appearance, I knew the vet might still recommend euthanasia. I held my breath and drove. As I led the dog into the veterinarian's waiting room, there was a collective audible gasp and then silence from those gathered there. I'd just entered with a living grinning canine skeleton draped in hot pink weeping skin, and scabs. One stunned person finally commandeered his dropped jaw, whistled softly, and asked, "What happened to that dog?"

What had happened? He had been burned. Brutally burned. Apparently with a liquid, suspected because of the path of the burn patterns over his protruding ribs and spine.

"Someone could have tossed hot oil on him or could have set him on fire," explained the vet.

Dumping boiling oil on the dog might have been a careless accident or a deliberate act of cruelty. Given the number of families around here who use outdoor fryers, and the number of burn injuries associated with these top-heavy, easily tipped appliances, I agree hot oil probably burned him, even by accident if the fryer was knocked over. I can never know for sure. But between the burns and mange and wiggly worms, it's little short of a miracle that the dog survived.

The vet gave him medicine for the mange, pills for the pain of his burns, a strong wormer medication by mouth, and we were off, both of us pleased he still had a heartbeat.

After a brief confinement for his treatment, the dog, now named Elliott, was released to play around my house and barn. Two weeks and 14 more pounds later, he was neutered and vaccinated. Elliott eventually tripled his weight to reach normal size. He's been adopted, and he lives in a lifetime home. SPF 100 sunblock is rubbed on his burn scars every morning and he has to wear a protective garment every day to keep the sun off of his back. Nevertheless, living in the intense summer sun of Mississippi, he still developed skin cancer on the bare burn scars on his back; it later metastasized to his bones. At age 11 he has far surpassed the age of his predicted demise from the cancer, and he continues to live a good life. I believe this is because of his positive attitude. He loves dogs, kids, cats, wildlife, the postman, the UPS driver, everyone. How, I'm not sure. Burns hurt. Elliott wouldn't hurt anyone. Starvation hurts. Elliott will share his food with anyone. Anytime.

We long ago discovered that pets are famous for their ability to forgive, to live in the moment, to not mope over past injuries or fret about future needs. Dogs eat the same dry processed food every day and are grateful for it. I groan about leftovers in my fridge. Dogs live in the moment. I regret the past and fret the future.

But I learned from Elliott: Every day take time to listen and learn from an animal. They have wisdom, galaxies beyond what we can imagine, that we must glean. Mining their data enriches our lives. Just sit with a cat on your lap and contemplate the purr. How do they do that? Why? Stroke your dog's head and wait for your blood pressure to settle. Watch your cat throw her tail in the air in salute as she approaches you; emulate her joy at seeing her friend. And try to be mindful like a dog for even a few minutes today: Don't worry about tomorrow, give thanks for your food, and for those who love you. Forgive those who have hurt you and accept apologies, even the ones you deserve that haven't been offered.

◆ ◆ ◆

Once a man called about getting his cat and her current litter fixed. When I went to get them for surgery, I found three 6-week-old summer kittens, and a four-pound juvenile cat I assumed was from the spring litter. I asked the owner to help me find the mother cat. He pointed to the juvenile. That diminutive teenage cat, not even a year old, not even an adult cat, was the mother of the three kittens. Fix by five to avoid this tragedy of kittens having kittens. (See fixbyfive.org for more info).

Paulette, named in honor of beloved animal welfare activist the late Paul Jolly

CHAPTER 3

Paulette

See something say something

WHEN AN ANIMAL welfare foundation gave us sturdy new dog houses for an elderly indigent woman's two dogs, we drove to her home on a dreary grey morning two days before Christmas to deliver them. Setting out the shelters, we helped fill them with hay and left with friendly hugs from the low-income owner.

The weather became more disagreeable as we returned on winding curves of a narrow blacktop county road, and I started the wipers when rain splattered rivulets of water across the windshield. Suddenly on the center line in the road in front of us there was something small, gray, and bloody. Forced to keep my eyes on the road to avoid hitting it, I didn't get a good look, but my fellow volunteer did. She works full-time, but called in 2002 to volunteer. Dedicated to reducing animal suffering and overpopulation, she's been advocating for animals for decades now.

"It's a cat I think," she said, turning in the seat to stare. "Should we go see?" she asked.

I didn't want to. Mangled animal = nightmare.

"Looked dead to me," I replied, having seen blood, but not really having had a good look either. "If we go back, you'll have to get out and look. I don't want to do that."

"I'll do it," she said.

Reversing course and returning to the scene, I pulled off the road into a driveway near the animal and started the flashers. Dashing out into the chilly rain, my colleague bent over the creature, then began to frantically wave.

"Alive," she shouted.

I reached into the back seat for the emergency animal rescue bag, a vinyl perforated bag used to secure and transport small animals in an emergency. I'd never used it before. Pulling my jacket tight against the brisk wind and stinging rain, I jogged back to her.

On the center line, hunched into a shaking, shivering wet ball of fur, was a cream, gray, and orange short-hair adult cat, a pastel tortoiseshell. Blood dripped steadily in a stream from her nose; her face and front paws red and sticky as it clotted and puddled on them. Clearly in shock, she seemed unaware of our presence. From her coloring, I knew we'd found a female; tortoiseshells and calicos are female.

How to proceed? Was the cat feral? Would she bite if I touched her? We had protective gloves, but anyone who's used those know they reduce your dexterity. It's not easy to handle a cat while you're wearing thick bulky welding gloves or protective animal-handling gloves. With the wind flapping my jacket like a sail, I decided to try to grab and drop the cat into the bag barehanded, then get us out of the middle of the road.

I stepped behind the cat while the other volunteer watched for traffic and held the bag open and ready. Scruffing the injured animal by the loose skin of her neck, I scooped up and supported her bottom with my other hand, then dunked her into the sack. She never resisted. We made a dash for the car, laid her on her side in the back, and cranked up the heat. We were about 25 miles from our veterinarian's clinic.

My colleague dashed to knock on the door of the home in front of the accident site, ignoring the "Day Sleeper Do Not Disturb" sign taped to the front door. I called our veterinarian's office.

"He's gone to do some Christmas shopping this morning," the receptionist said.

"Find him please, it's an emergency, this cat is critically injured," I explained. "We're on our way in with her."

On the drive my friend recounted the conversation with the man of that house. Yes, they had cats, no he didn't know if that one was theirs, no it didn't matter if it was, no he wasn't coming out in the rain to look, and no it did not matter to him whether we took her or she died. He closed the door. Whatever happened at this point then, she belonged to us.

Standing at the door waiting to receive the bloody bundle when the cat arrived, the veterinarian immediately began rewarming her and started an intravenous drip to replace lost blood. She had a fractured femur, broken jaw, ruptured eardrum, and several teeth had been knocked out.

"She may also be blind," he noted. "But there's no way to tell until she regains consciousness."

Paulette three days after her accident

Is this a feral cat who will wake up terrified? If so, we'd likely need to consider a painful decision to euthanize her. Ferals are absolutely always worthy of medical care, but if providing care stresses and terrorizes the cat, then is that kind and compassionate? Sometimes you have to decide who you're doing this for.

That decision never had to be made. The cat regained consciousness, clearly hadn't been blinded, and certainly wasn't feral. She loved to be petted and she purred on contact. Her leg was set in a splint. With her ear drained, she regained excellent hearing. Her jaw healed quickly and she never missed the teeth.

We could not, of course, put her back out at the home near where we'd found her. When she was discharged from the hospital, I took her home to "foster" her. "Foster" and "adopt" are typically synonymous in the South. You should acknowledge that when you pick up a stray animal: The person who puts the animal in their car is most likely the person who will be paying its veterinary bills, caring for it, and providing a home. With few adopters available, I had little hope of placing her. I tried though, and never got the first nibble of interest.

She became my treasure. We named her Paulette, after Paul Jolly, then the director of The PETCO Foundation, which gave us the dog houses. Beloved nationwide in the animal welfare community, Paul had been a hands-on animal welfare advocate himself before accepting his leadership role at PETCO. He was a true treasure to animal welfare advocates and the animals themselves; he always made our work helping animals easier, never harder. Since his passing, he has been sorely missed. Without those dog houses he'd granted, we wouldn't have been in that area, and we wouldn't have happened upon Paulette. The cat likely would have died there in the road, shivering and bleeding in the rain and cold wind. But Paulette lived another 15 years with us as a prized friend and family companion.

The lesson? When you see a cat or dog in or near the road who's obviously injured, assess the situation for the safety of yourself and others first, but do consider stopping to help. I suspected this cat was dead and might have kept going if my companion hadn't suggested otherwise. Thank goodness she taught me that lesson early on.

A couple of rules, of course: Can you get to the animal without reasonably endangering yourself or others? You can elect to risk martyring yourself, but you are not allowed to risk others' lives if you decide to step onto a roadway to get to an animal. You must also accept and even expect that a frightened and hurting cat or dog may bite or injure you, which means you're the one going to the emergency room. *You* know you're trying to help the animal; the animal doesn't. So always approach with caution. Do not attempt to handle an injured or hurting animal without considering the consequences to your health and safety first. Obviously the larger the animal, the greater the risk to the rescuer.

Call a wildlife center if you encounter injured wildlife, do not attempt to intervene without their guidance. Wildlife care is usually regulated by state or federal laws. Wildlife experts recommend not attempting to "rescue" or intervene with baby deer, rabbits, and many fledgling birds who are not obviously injured, because their mothers often leave them unattended and are typically nearby. Always call an expert first when wildlife is involved. Type "wildlife rehab" and your zip code into an internet search engine for suggestions.

If you do stop to help and find the creature is already deceased, at least you know there's no more suffering. If you reach an animal who is mortally wounded but alive, you may be able to get him to a vet for swift relief of the suffering. Be prepared to pay for professional services, although the fee for emergency euthanasia of a suffering stray animal should be basic and not exorbitant. In rural areas you typically will be expected to take the remains with you for burial.

Incredibly, you may find an animal who's only been stunned—knocked unconscious briefly—but can get up and go on her way with your help. Since that day, I have stopped to check on downed animals, sometimes with happy outcomes, sometimes without. It's difficult. But please try. It may be the difference between suffering, life, or death for an animal.

Countless cats may surrender or even relax when scruffed. The scruff is the skin over the nape of the neck. Mother cats carry their kittens by the scruff of their necks, and a male cat grabs the female's scruff when breeding, so it is not an unfamiliar sensation to a cat. To scruff a cat, open your fingers wide around the nape of the neck, then close your fist, pulling up on the skin. When you scruff a cat, watch for their ears to rotate back as you pull up on the scruff; if the cat's ears pull back with your grip, your hand is in a good position to reduce your risk of a bite. Do not grab that loose skin further back over the cat's shoulder blades. It's not a comforting sensation for a cat, and it allows the cat the freedom to whip his head around to bite your grip hand. Grip further forward and watch the ears pull back to insure you're in a good position. Always use your other hand to scoop up and support the cat's hindquarters and full weight as you dunk the animal into a waiting crate, cage, or rescue bag. You'll find this technique preferable and less stressful on both you and the cat than trying to force a scared cat face-first into a crate or carrier. If you are bitten by a cat, wash the wound and seek medical attention immediately, not hours or days later.

Feral cat Gotcha after relocation

CHAPTER 4

Gotcha

Fast food ferals

WE ROUTINELY RECEIVE calls about feral cat colonies; most callers want us to remove the cats and "find them good homes." Of course, by definition a feral cat isn't a pet. If the caller is willing to allow the cats to live there and agrees to monitor and feed the colony daily (about half the callers will commit) we will provide traps and trapping assistance, and our vet will provide the spay or neuter surgery and a rabies vaccination. Spay/neuter surgery groups and humane organizations generally remove the tip of a feral cat's left ear while they are asleep for the surgery. This universal sign lets vets, animal control officers, residents, and caregivers know the cat has been sterilized. Ear tipping can save a female cat from a second exploratory surgery to determine if she's been spayed. We encourage the procedure for feral and free roaming community cats.

A woman, I'll call her Jane, rang us about three cats living behind a fast food restaurant. She was feeding them nightly, but was rightly concerned for their safety and feared their reproduction.

When I spoke with the manager of the fast food restaurant, he quickly granted permission to trap. Permission to return them didn't come as quickly. I hoped to relocate these cats because they were landlocked not far from a busy intersection with 16 total lanes of traffic controlled by a dozen traffic signals swaying overhead. Unsafe territory. Seeking shelter in a drain pipe, they had inadequate cover in foul weather. However, the manager agreed, as most do, that if I couldn't find a barn or property to take them it would be better to have them trapped, neutered, and returned than to remain fertile on the property.

Because of the distance from our base, we had to rely on Jane to perform the trapping. She did, and she caught all of the cats, including Gotcha. It took weeks of her sitting in her car in that dark parking lot between 11:00 pm and 2:00 am, but she caught the cats. The most elusive, in the photo, was the last to be caught. The trapper dubbed her "Gotcha" when she caught her. Upon spay, it was discovered that Gotcha's womb held mummified kittens. Obstetric complications occur in cats and dogs, just like in humans. Had she not been trapped for surgery, the dead kittens in her uterus would have slowly and painfully killed her; I refuse to think about what that belly felt like to her. It's unbearable to consider.

What I learned from Gotcha: That which is not easily treated had better be prevented. It is exponentially easier and cheaper to fix a few cats before the reproduction starts, than to wait until there is even one litter to try to catch and fix. Jane dedicated numerous nights to trapping these three cats; imagine how many dozens of cats there would be just months later if she had not.

Make trapping and sterilization a priority when you discover a colony of unmanaged ferals. First, contact the property owner. You'll need permission to be on the property for trapping and permission to return the cats after they've been fixed and recovered. Securing this in writing is best.

Trap divider confines cat in position for anesthetic injection

Next, you need someone who can commit to daily feeding/watering of the colony. In cold weather, someone will have to break up frozen water. And you need a vet who is able to treat a feral cat when needed. An essential tool for all feral cat vets is a trap divider, a fork-like metal device you can push through the wires of the trap. Forcing the cat into one corner of the trap, the vet can inject a sedative and then easily examine and treat the cat once she loses consciousness. The cat is returned to the trap for recovery. None of us has ever been injured by a feral cat, because we only handle them when they are unconscious. If you have a feral who needs treatment, make sure your vet has experience in this.

Gotcha and the other two cats were successfully relocated, and nearly a year later are living out their lives in a rural barn. I learned from Gotcha that perseverance pays off, and there are people, good people, in our communities who will sacrifice their time to reduce animal suffering.

We cared for a feral cat who lived behind a commercial building in a small town; volunteers took turns dropping off food and water daily after we had him neutered and vaccinated. One day a new resident discovered the cat and started feeding him. But this person made a fuss: Pulled up on the street at noon, threw open all car doors, set a 20-pound bag of cat food on the sidewalk, and proceeded to fill bowls, which were not retrieved after feeding. Raccoons, opossums, and stray dogs discovered the food site and frequented the area. It wasn't long before the cat was found dead. We'll never know what happened, but we suspect that public awareness of the cat's presence along with the excess cat food and paper bowls littering the ground caused animosity towards him. The cat may have been poisoned to stop the feeding. If you discover feral cats, check to see if a tip of the cats' ears has been removed. Generally, the tip of the left ear is removed, as in the photo, when a feral cat comes in for surgery. Scout around for water bowls. If ear-tipped cats appear well fed and healthy, it's best to stand down with skillful observation and patience while you discreetly determine if they are a managed colony.

Left ear tip removed indicates cat is sterile

CHAPTER 5

Emma

Own the oath

"MY CAT HAS been in labor since Saturday night," the caller said at 8:00 am on Monday morning. "It's been about 36-hours. She's nearly dead, and I think she needs to be put to sleep. It's awful seeing Emma like this, but I don't have the money to pay the vet."

The stray pregnant gray-tabby long-hair cat had appeared at this woman's home about one month earlier. Immediately a hit with the kids, especially the woman's daughter, the cat quickly bonded with the family. Two days ago, on Saturday night the caller said, the cat's labor had started. Through the night the cat strained but pushed nothing from her womb. Sunday morning, this woman called the nearest veterinary clinic's emergency number. Her call was returned, but when she admitted she did not have the $100 emergency fee, the vet refused to see the cat.

Suffering on through Sunday, the cat tired and began to fail. Still no kittens, but one could see the ripples of her uterine contractions straining to push out the uterine contents. On Monday morning, desperate to relieve the beloved cat's suffering, the owner called a nearby veterinary clinic, also owned by the initial vet she'd talked with Sunday, and explained the situation. No mercy. The usual weekday charge for the cat to be seen in the clinic by a vet would be $45, cash in advance, and the owner still didn't have that money. So she called us.

"She's nearly dead now, barely breathing, she's not moving. We have to do something!"

"Do you have a car?" I asked. She did. She had gas in it, and the car was roadworthy enough to make it to our veterinarian's clinic. I'd learned early on that just because someone had a car didn't mean it qualified as transportation or that it would make it more than a few miles.

"Put the cat in the car, immediately, and go directly to this clinic," I told her, giving her and address. "This is an emergency. Go. Go now."

Calling our veterinarian, I relayed the information. We agreed that the cat likely was beyond anything other than euthanasia. About an hour later he called me.

"Uterus ruptured. All the kittens are dead, she had a bad infection setting in. Cat was moribund, but still, she's young. I took out what remained of her uterus. Got her cleaned out good. I put her on antibiotics. I don't know if she'll make it or not. We'll see," he said.

Each day that cat improved. On Tuesday she sat up. On Wednesday she began to eat. By Thursday she was stable and standing. On Saturday, she was discharged. I picked her up, paid the vet bill, which was modest in comparison to the care provided, and drove Emma toward her home.

At a distance, it seemed too nice of a home for someone unable to come up with $45 for emergency euthanasia and I felt resentment and cynicism budding in my gut. But when I reached the end of the long driveway, I spotted the disrepair: shingles missing, broken windows, rotting sills, sagging gutters. Overgrown brush obscured the walk. These are common signs of job loss, family breakup, diminishing health, or advancing age. Emma's owner opened a creaking front door, revealing a chilly house nearly devoid of furniture. She offered an embarrassed apology.

"I'm raising the children alone. We don't have very much anymore," she said softly. The children stood shyly behind her, eagerly peering beyond me at the pet crate. Kneeling, I released the pet carrier door. Emma stepped out, sized up her surroundings, saw her favorite little girl, and trotted over to her. The child dropped to the floor, opened her arms, and Emma circled then curled into the child's lap. So dear, so sweet, so strong, the bond between animals and those they love! Tears welled in my eyes and my heart swelled to witness this reunion. This previously homeless 6-pound feline comforted and nurtured a child hurting from loss and separation and in the process gave the child hope and returned some of the love that she needed.

The lesson? The veterinary oath states that veterinarians will use their scientific knowledge and skills for the prevention and relief of animal suffering. Understandably professionals expect to be paid for their services. But when faced with a clear emergency, nearly all professionals—whether involved in animal welfare or human—step up and do what needs to be done that immediate moment to save a life or alleviate suffering. Regretfully, not every professional honors their oath.

The doctor who saved Emma lives his oath every day though. He didn't just relieve her suffering. He fought her battle for her, when she was exhausted and near death. When she could fight it no more, he kept fighting for her. That's a real veterinarian. That's the kind we have helping us, and the kind you want for your animals. So, if your vet is strictly a businessperson, consider a switch. When your pets need care, choose a vet who has compassion, who knows the magnitude of animal overpopulation and the attendant suffering. Choose one who is proactive against animal suffering and overpopulation through spay/neuter, and is committed to using his or her skills and training to alleviate animal suffering. That's the person you want battling for your animal's life, and for all the animals of the world. That's the person we want to support.

When pet owners call to schedule spay/neuter surgery for a pet, always ask, "Now what about your other pets?" There are usually more, but they haven't been mentioned because owners often care only about getting their female pets fixed, or they don't want a purebred "high blood" purchased animal fixed.

If we're providing free or very low-cost care, we do not allow them to choose which of their pets will be fixed and which will be left fertile. We schedule the male pets for surgery first, then once that is accomplished, we'll schedule the females. If owners get their female pets fixed first, we won't hear from them again because they believe they've solved their problem.

However, customers will foil our plan by showing up with female animals instead, claiming they couldn't find the males that day. It's frustrating so be prepared.

April staring

CHAPTER 6

April

Lineman to the rescue

"I HEARD THIS meowing, and I went over to look. There was a cat in the grass. She stood up when I got to her. I mean, she tried to stand. She kept going right back down. There's something wrong with her leg, and her tail is all messed up," explained the caller late one April afternoon. A contract utility worker, he'd been working the wires along Interstate 55 in northern Mississippi when he discovered a calico cat who'd obviously been hit by a car. "I went and got her some cat food on my lunch break, and I gave her some of my water, but I can't keep her. I can't take her with me. I hope you will help her. I've been calling everybody I could think of. Nobody will take her, they're full, or I'll have to pay for everything and keep her, and I can't do that."

After giving me a detailed description of the location where he last saw the injured cat, he disconnected. One of our volunteers drove to the scene, found the cat in the tall grass by the Interstate, and chauffeured her to our veterinarian, who called later that evening.

"This is a young female cat, hit by car. Her tail has to come off, and she's got some damage to her hind leg. But she's a real sweet cat, just real nice," he reported.

I agreed to cover the cost of the tail amputation and the spay, and of course, I couldn't place her. Everybody who wants a cat or a dog already has one. I didn't have a vacancy for a housecat at the time, and didn't even want another house pet, yet I could take another outdoor cat if I had to. My spirits sank when a few days later I brought this exquisite calico cat home and found that while she could stand, with weight-bearing her right rear paw crumpled under her and the leg wobbled. Nerve damage, the vet explained. Might get better, he said. But no way could this cat live outdoors without four firm legs. I'd have to keep her inside until her leg strengthened, if it ever did.

Eleven years later, we'd have a bare-knuckled brawl before I'd let you take this dear creature out of my house or my sight. A prize she is, a graceful compassionate creature who is the plush and tangible gift of love known as a cat. With delicate pink nose leather and soft white fuzz in her black-ringed ears, she has a glossy luxurious coat painted with bright splashes of orange and white blended with black to create that classic calico look, and those large round green eyes. Her leg is mostly healed, although she still has a little weakness and her knee will hyperextend when she stretches. April loves to play fetch. I buy her favorite toy at a discount store in bulk so she'll always have a fresh one when the old one wears out. She follows me everywhere. Wherever I am, that is where April is. She stares at me and purrs. Just sits and stares and purrs. It's disconcerting, because she is as captivated by me as I am by her. Why do our pets stare at us? I am convinced it is more than food they are thinking about when they follow us and watch us and stare at us.

Admire the beauty of the creature admiring you right now. Your cardiovascular system, your immune system, and your nervous system all benefit from basking in that dazzling beauty and in that admiring gaze, even if just for a few minutes. That's a fact, and that's the lesson she taught me. Stop, look, and be dazzled. Help a downed animal today, and she or he will lift you up tomorrow.

A woman called, wanting six feral cats removed from her yard. I explained we had no place for them to go and extolled the virtues of trap–neuter–return (TNR), telling her the reproduction would stop, and the fighting and other unpleasant behaviors would be dramatically reduced. Disgruntled that I wouldn't catch and remove the cats, she did agree to TNR. I trapped six cats, took them for surgery, and recovered them overnight. Parking in front of her home the following morning, I began releasing the cats. She summoned the police, claiming she had no idea who I was or why I was dumping wild cats on her property. Best to get it in writing.

Rocky soaking up sun

CHAPTER 7

Rocky

Fake it 'til you make it

DRIVING TO A Blessing of the Pets ceremony one October, I saw a kitten wobbling and falling on the dirt shoulder of pot-hole pitted road that passed through a rural low-income neighborhood. About six weeks old, the yellow tabby short-hair male clearly had hind end trouble: His pelvis swayed and tilted side to side as he tottered on unsteady back legs. Sometimes his hips just rocked to and fro, sometimes his hindquarters lost the balance battle and took him to the ground. Popping back up unfazed, the kitten continued his teeter-totter gait across the road. Frightened for his safety, I parked my car and grabbed him. Cradling the one-pound creature in my hand, I queried a woman nearby in a carport: Know anything about this kitten?

No, she said, she had seen him wobbling around the area, figured something was wrong with him, but didn't believe he belonged to anyone. Expressing concern for his condition, she admitted she didn't know what to do. You're thinking, "take him to a vet" but I've met people who wonder "what's a vet?" Most of those in our community who do know what a vet is also know when they cannot afford one. Others simply would never, even with money in their pocket, consider spending it on a cat: If that one dies, there are plenty more.

Putting the cheerful, diminutive kitten into a crate and driving him to receive his blessing, I despaired it might be a type of last rites. Flopping is definitely a discouraging prognostic sign. Would euthanasia be recommended? After his blessing, we went to the veterinary clinic. As we waited to see the doctor, I fretted over his future.

Introducing himself to everyone there though, the light-hearted little fellow flip-flopped around the waiting room. Toppling over, he'd right himself, wobble a few more steps, fall over, get up, fall over, get up. In the process of this he tumbled into the hearts of everyone there.

After an exam revealed no abnormalities, the vet gave him a dose of steroids and started him on an antibiotic. "I'll keep him a week and see how he does. We can always put him down later if he doesn't get better."

Rocky didn't improve much that week, but who could euthanize such a cheerful, charming, captivating pint-size creature? Upon discharge he came to my home, and because of his unsteadiness I confined him to one bedroom. There he taught himself to stay upright more consistently by straightening his tail and holding it stiff against a vertical surface, usually the wall. Using his tail as a sort of upside-down rigid cane to steady his pelvis and hips, he'd lean his weight into the wall or furniture in order to walk without falling. Of course, this required him to stay alongside vertical surfaces; if he tried to cross the middle of a room he wobbled and tumbled again, but finally he got to the point where he was strong enough to avoid most falls. That took about six months. Around 10 months of age he was stable enough to go outdoors some during the day. While I absolutely agree all cats are safest and healthiest living indoors, I do not have the capacity to house them all in my home. As I live on a large acreage in a rural area, I do keep some cats outdoors.

Once he could walk without falling, Rocky began to try running. But his hindquarter instability would surface at speed, and you would see his hips swaying back and forth as he moved faster. He didn't fall though, and by the time he was two, Rocky was completely normal in gait and lifestyle. We suspect his mother contracted distemper when pregnant, and thus the remainder of the litter likely died along with her, while Rocky lived. Because he survived, he was immune to distemper after that.

Although he died rather young of heart failure at age 13, Rocky ranks as the happiest creature I've ever met in my whole life: He was always cheerful and always happy to make your acquaintance. Rocky never swatted or hissed at anyone, 2-legged or 4-legged. A lesson I learned from Rocky is always shine with your best attitude to keep the folks in charge smiling, then work every angle you can to meet your goals. I learned to be adaptable too. Rocky adapted by holding his tail rigid and using it for support so that he would not fall, until he didn't need the support of his tail any longer and could sashay around, curling and furling it in greeting. I am glad I didn't superimpose my values (how terrible it must be to fall with each step) and that I let him work it out himself. Rocky underwent an amazing transformation and transition. I am mightily privileged and blessed to have witnessed him adapt and thrive. With his cheerful pleasant personality, Rocky was easy to care for; because of his good cheer and his resourcefulness in learning to walk and run, euthanasia was unwarranted. Be adaptable, like Rocky, and don't swat at or hiss at other people. Be so cheerful, pleasant, flexible, persevering, and friendly that no one wants to put you down either.

You can't catch that cat," they'll say, walking away from you, shaking their heads at your stupidity. But you can catch that cat. Humane traps come in all shapes and sizes. We mostly use Tru Catch Tuffy 24 traps because of their small size and light-weight (less than five pounds), plus the brown color helps camouflage them when set in public areas. Larger Tru Catch traps are available, including ones with a guillotine style back door. At your local hardware store, you'll find heavier, larger traps; these give the target cat more room, but can be hard to carry with an angry thrashing tomcat inside. Sometimes a wary cat requires a double-door trap that it can see straight through. Large cats may need larger traps that don't feel so confined. There are also tiny kitten traps that trigger more easily when little ones enter, and finally, drop traps. A drop trap is a large cage-like box that is propped up with a support which is connected to a string. Food is slipped under the cage. When the target cat enters, the trapper yanks the string and the trap drops over the cat. A smaller transfer cage is affixed to the side, and the cat is shooed into the transfer cage for the trip to the vet. One trap doesn't work? There is another one that will. If you can control the food and keep dogs or onlookers away, you are likely going to get the cat. Especially if you stop first for some hot fast food boneless fried chicken as bait.

Feral cat entering trap

Barney one week later

CHAPTER 8

Barney

Size matters

A CALLER ON a weekday morning reported seeing two dogs abandoned in a driveway on the highway leading out of our town.

"Truck pulled over, guy gets out, reaches in the back, yanks out two dogs by their collars, and tosses them down. Throws it in reverse and he's gone," she said.

Because she was traveling to work, the caller explained she could not be late and thus did not stop after she witnessed the dump.

When there are no shelters, when the nearest shelter euthanizes excess animals, or when there is a fee to surrender an unwanted pet, irresponsible pet owners may drive the animals to a park or rural farm area and abandon them. Churches, schools, and shopping centers are popular dump spots too, anywhere that women and children frequent. People who have abandoned pets on public property claim "at least he has a chance here." Abandoned dogs may sit for days waiting for their ride to return. Cats will typically flee in terror into the nearest woods to never be seen again.

Driving to the spot where the dogs were abandoned, I averted my eyes from the sight when I realized one had already been hit and killed. Standing near the remains, the second dog seemed confused and perplexed as to why his friend remained motionless. A dirty gray color with a tangled and matted coat, the male mixed-breed, about 15 pounds, retreated toward an abandoned barn on the unoccupied property when I approached him. Setting a trap, I quickly secured him. But as I approached fleas jumped from the dog to my legs and feet, blackening my ankles and feet with their sheer numbers. Stomping and kicking, I fled to the car for flea spray. Once we were both doused with it, I loaded the dog into my car.

With the help of a kind vet, the dog was bathed and clipped and returned home with me a new man. Neutered a week later, Barney was offered for adoption and he promptly had a new indoor home. The first week there he destroyed new window blinds, but his owner had already fallen in love and thankfully she laughed about it when I made a follow-up call.

Barney taught me traps aren't just for cats; sometimes dogs need a trap too, and most of the time it's just because they are scared, not actually wild. However, a dog who is so insecure that he will never approach you or allow you to touch him could be dangerous to you. Obviously, if you decide to approach an unknown dog, do it with caution, if at all. Calling Animal Control is typically the best option, if you have that service in your area. In my area we do not. Do not risk injury or your life by trying to force care on a frightened, injured, or cornered dog who is warning you to stay away (growling, aggressive posturing, snapping, barking) or running from you.

If you are able to safely approach a friendly stray dog, you may be able to slip a noose type slip lead over its head. Then snug it slightly on the neck, and gently loop the remaining part of the leash around the dog's muzzle. This will reduce the chance of being bitten while you lift the dog into your car or crate. Lowering your face to an unknown dog's face can be dangerous; you are risking severe or even fatal injury. Maybe the dog will not bite, but if he or she does, it could be bad. Don't make yourself vulnerable.

If you witness animal abandonment, try to get the vehicle's license plate number and report it to the local police and animal shelter. If it is safe to do so, secure the animal in a crate or on a leash before taking the creature to a shelter.

I also learned from Barney that a grooming session cheers woman and beast alike. And I learned that in dog adoptions, size matters. Barney was small. Small opens doors. As dog size increases, the pool of potential adopters plummets. The public seem to prefer small dogs, and sometimes their living quarters dictate that. Large dogs cost more to maintain and certainly require increased exercise and room. It's just a lot harder to place big dogs in an already competitive market. Celebrities with pocket pets have made it harder too, as admirers want a small dog like that. Big dogs are good dogs too though.

Barney when abandoned

*Feral cats in a quiet area awaiting surgery, off the floor,
covered, although drape was removed for photo.*

Cover caged, trapped, or crated cats with a towel, sheet, or drape to reduce their fright. Cats stress easily, which makes them vulnerable to illness, plus it's simply humane to help them feel less terrified when confined. Once you've trapped a feral cat, immediately drape the trap with a sheet or towel and remove the cat to a safe, quiet location until transport. When possible, store confined cats off the ground, up on shelving or table tops. Cats are natural climbers and feel less threatened when elevated off the ground.

CHAPTER 9

Lindacee

One at a time

IT WAS LATE afternoon when I pulled off the interstate after a tiresome workday. I eased into the lineup of rush hour traffic and rolled under the interstate bridge. As the tractor trailer in front of me lurched forward, I spotted the tiny black ears of a kitten lying at the edge of the road. Or was it a black garbage bag? A kitten wouldn't be resting that close to the road at an interstate interchange. At least not a live one. I must have seen a garbage bag. I kept going.

But what if it was a kitten, maybe alive, baking in the summer heat in that deadly location? She or he certainly couldn't survive long. A half-mile down the road I decided I had to be sure, so I reversed course and passed under the interstate again. Stopped traffic blocked my view. Finally headed in the right direction after another 180-degree about face, I sighed with relief when I spotted a black garbage bag. That is, until I saw the kitten, about 8 weeks old, beyond the garbage bag. Covered with dirt and gravel, the solid black short-hair feline appeared dead, but then I witnessed the flick of an ear again. Tires of 18-wheelers and cars rumbled by just inches from her, and I had to look away.

With no place to safely stop, I made a third pass. Waiting for traffic to clear, I decided to whip into the turning lane, start the flashers, and slip through the stalled traffic to snatch her up. As I reached for the kitten, she lifted her head and gave me a resigned look that seemed to say *I don't know what you want lady, but I'm having a really bad day here, and I don't need any more trouble.* I grabbed the limp little body, swiped off the blanket of ants that swarmed over her, and jogged back to my idling car.

Setting her down on the floorboard, I pulled out of traffic. In the nearest parking lot, I examined the dull-coated kitten, but only after opening my car door, hanging her out, and knocking the rest of those ants off of her. With that she snuggled into the crook of my arm and purred, although she cried out in pain when I touched her right hind leg. Her eyes met mine just once as she stole a furtive glimpse of me, like she was wondering whether this turn of events was good or bad.

After a veterinary exam, we put the kitten on cage rest at my home, and while she ate hungrily, she seemed depressed, lying quietly, purring when touched but otherwise silent. Non-weight bearing on the right hind leg at first, she began ambulating normally within three days. The veterinarian recommended rest and time, and sure enough, within a week she morphed into a charming, engaged kitten. Exploring, tumbling, and playing, her depressed affect vanished. Three weeks later the now shiny and spayed sweetheart had a forever home with a friend of mine, where she is much loved.

The lesson I learned? You have time to check on a downed animal, one who may be suffering, no matter how inconvenient it may be. It only takes a few minutes to see if they are alive or dead. I saved only one creature this afternoon when there were millions suffering, but...one sweet, tender heartbeat at a time is the only way most of us will ever be able to help animals.

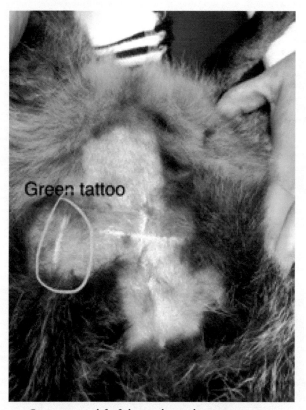

Green tattoo on left of photo indicates this is a spay incision

Some veterinarians apply a line of tattoo ink near their spay incision of pet cats. If the cat is lost or trapped, a shave of the belly indicates that surgical scar is from a spay surgery, not some other procedure, and we know there is no need to re-operate.

CHAPTER 10

Shirley

Arachnids & ammunition

ABOUT TWO MONTHS after we moved to Mississippi, I stepped outdoors one spring morning to discover a cream-colored female dog, about 45 pounds, sitting at our back door. She had a hearty Lab-dog type torso with short, stubby legs, like a Basset Hound. Our eyes met. She grinned, then flipped belly up in a charming demonstration of trust, offering friendship to me. Kneeling in grass damp with dew to stroke her, I recoiled when firm pebble or marble-like objects rippled under my hands. I parted her thick inch-long fur to find not marbles but engorged ticks. Hard, shiny, taut and swollen rigid, the ticks were nearly bursting with her blood. The dog had these greenish-gray arachnids embedded in every inch of skin, from her nose, eyes, and lips to her genitals and the tip of her tail. She rolled gentle golden-brown eyes up at me and remained quiet on the ground as I examined her. Returning to the house, I poured a quart of alcohol into an old gallon pail, pulled on disposable gloves, and returned to the dog. Patient and cooperative, she let me pick the ticks off, one by one. I had to work in short shifts, frequently standing to rest my knees. Over an hour later I had a backache but the dog had no ticks. I finished with an application of topical tick and flea preventive.

As this dog was gentle and friendly, I hoped she could be placed in an adoptive home. Calling a new neighbor, I asked how to reach the area animal shelter.

That's when I discovered to my surprise, at least in 1996, that neither the city nor the county had an animal shelter or animal control officer. No humane society or animal rescue organizations either.

"Well what do you do when a stray dog shows up?" I asked.

"You can shoot it yourself, or you can call the Sheriff. They'll shoot it for you, if you don't want to keep it."

Of course, we didn't shoot her; we kept her. Named for our beloved pastor, Shirley was spayed and vaccinated, then became a treasured pet who lived with us for 13 years. Loving the water, she clearly had some Lab in her, and her mottled blue tongue spoke highly of Chow. Unfazed by the cold through her now thick coat, she would come running to the house with icicles clinking an upbeat musical tune after a paddle through the pond in freezing weather. As she aged, she spent her days loafing under a majestic maple tree near the house. Digging a cavity that just fit her shape in the dirt, she slumbered there for hours on hot summer days. A year after her death, the wind blew a bird's nest from that tree. In the center I discovered a soft cushioned bed for the chicks made from Shirley's fur, gathered by a bird from the ground around that loafing spot. Who could witness this nest and not stand in awe of a bird who can, without hands, construct such a sturdy but fluffy cradle for her offspring? Woven throughout the nest were strands of our horses' manes and tails, too. I secured the nest under glass in my home; I treasure the joy Shirley gave us during her life, and I wonder at the art and architecture of bird nest building every time I see it.

From Shirley I learned that not everyone has the advantage of an animal shelter, humane society or animal control officer in their community. When there's no one assigned to help the animals, we have to do it ourselves. But we should also hound our elected representatives and demand they explain why we have no humane shelter for homeless or stray animals, and no humane animal officer. Support the modest tax increase that provides these critical services for animals and your community.

You can judge a people and their community, and even a whole country, by how they treat the least and most vulnerable among them.

◆ ◆ ◆

One older lady explained she didn't want her cat spayed, because she delighted in seeing kittens playing outside her kitchen window every spring. While kittens in the spring are a charming sight, these are sentient beings who as living creatures have the ability, like us, to suffer, therefore it is unconscionable to treat them as entertainment while ignoring the needs they have in common with us. She disagreed that animals suffer or feel pain. But after a stilted debate, she did allow me to take her cat for spay surgery, at my expense. I did, and it was worth it.

CHAPTER 11

Victor

Ferals flee

I DIDN'T KNOW a lot about feral cats when I saw a segment about them on the local TV in 1997. A property owner in a nearby town, who also happened to be a top city official, had ordered the animal control officer to shoot to death the cats roaming his business property. The officer complied, but his gunfire drew the attention of a homeowner nearby. Following the noise, the woman found six cats already deceased and others wounded. She confronted the officer and halted the abominable, outrageously cruel and heinous crusade. Wrathful community outrage followed. The animal control officer was fired, but the elected official who ordered the killing never faced charges or impeachment. The surviving feral cats were successfully trapped and fixed, but they needed new homes, as this man clearly was capable of cruelty and the cats could not safely remain there.

I agreed to take one cat for our barn. A lovely short-hair tuxedo cat with a white chin, chest, and snow-white paws, he huddled for three weeks terrified in a crate installed in a large cage in our barn. The crate enables the cat to hide and thus feel less vulnerable while confined in the larger cage. It is disturbing to see a petrified cat cowering in a box in a cage for that period; it is tedious work cleaning a litter box and feeding/watering a wild cat every day, all while trying to keep him from escaping the cage.

Once released though, this cat found happiness. He lived out his 14-year life in our barn. Named Victor because he won his battle with this barbarian, the cat grew into a majestic, stately creature. A busy hunter, he kept snakes and mice out of the horse feed and the barn. Late one night I happened to be in the barn checking on a horse when he came backing in the door, dragging a rat almost as big as himself.

For the man who wanted Victor dead, the one who put out the hit on him, I photographed the cat. Then, every year of Victor's life, on the anniversary of the slaughter, I sent the brute an updated photo postcard of Victor. On it I wrote messages like "Victor is doing great! Keeping the barn clear and safe for us! Great cat." Every card had a reminder that trap-neuter-return is the efficient, decent, humane option for managing feral cats; it is more effective than cruelty to reduce their colony numbers.

Truly feral, Victor never allowed us to touch him. As he aged, his coat dulled, and he lost weight. By then we'd opened a bedroom in our home to aging barn cats, for the ones who had gone deaf or blind or had become so arthritic that it was unsafe for them to live outdoors. It's known as assisted living. At age 14, Victor met criteria for admission, but we could not catch him. Until one day he didn't hear us approach, and we were able to scoop him up into a crate, quickly sedate him, and let the vet release him peacefully from this life. During his lifetime with us he was no trouble. We merely fed, housed, and admired him.

Victor was my first feral cat. From him I learned feral cats are either cats born in the wild or pet cats who were abandoned or lost, and without human contact, return to being wild and untamed. Most were born homeless and thus never socialized, so they will spend their lives fearful of humans. Feral cats do not attack people, they flee from humans; no one need fear ferals, they fear you more. Once sterilized, feral cats typically remain in their area and protect their domicile from rodents, reptiles, and interlopers. With food, water, and shelter, they live out the lives they've been given in peace, with restful hours in the sunlight. Because ferals are difficult to relocate, as a general rule they should not be, unless it is unavoidable. For example, if a deserted building where they live is to be demolished. Or cats living in a drainage ditch under a major traffic intersection, cats who have been threatened, and cats who have no established caregivers. Cats neither wanted nor tolerated where they are should be considered for relocation if a truce cannot be reached. Trapping a feral, having the cat spayed or neutered by a vet, and then returning it to its territory is referred to as trap-neuter-return, or TNR.

Feral colonies can be sterilized, managed, and their numbers will naturally diminish with their life cycles. To identify the cat as sterile and vaccinated, the tip of the cat's left ear is removed during their sterilization surgery. It's their instant ID and assists caregivers, animal control officers, or vets in determining who's been fixed and who's a newcomer. Most feline experts recommend not attempting to tame or socialize adult feral cats; it is unlikely to be successful, will stress the cat, and you are going to be scratched or bitten. If you want to know more about feral cats, search the term on the internet and enjoy reading about these elusive and hardy beauties.

Feral cat Gotcha in her orientation cage

Feral cats ideally should be maintained in their existing location. However, circumstances sometimes require relocation. Feral cats being relocated must be confined for at least three weeks in a large cage in their new location. Truly wild cats could require longer confinement, up to five weeks. The cage should be big enough that the cat can jump and move around freely, and should contain a crate or box for hiding to reduce the cat's stress. Caged ferals must be in a safe location where dogs, children, or adversaries absolutely cannot get at them. If a cat stops hiding or cowering in the crate when fed and watered, you might consider release at 3-4 weeks. If the cat approaches you, vocalizes, and makes eye contact, you can consider release earlier. Every time I put a feral cat through relocation and witness their frustration in the cage and face the responsibility of keeping their cages clean and their water bowls upright, I question the decision I made for the cat. And every time after I release them and see them frolicking in their new home, I give thanks I stuck it out with them. Three to five weeks of detention to give a feral cat a chance at a lifetime of peaceful, safe living is worth it if they must be relocated.

CHAPTER 12

The Hoarder

Too much of a good thing

ONE AUGUST MORNING in 1999 a caller explained that her mother collected cats but there were so many she was now unable to care for them. After their trailer became nearly uninhabitable due to cat soiling, her mother began storing the felines in an outdoor pen and tin shed. As often happens in overcrowding, the caller reported many of the cats to be ill and underfed. Although this woman didn't want her mother to know she'd reported the situation, she gave me her mother's phone number. I called the collector, who made it clear she wasn't going to accept our help with fixing the cats or any other intervention. She refused to speak with me again.

Phoning rescue organizations and animal welfare contacts, I discovered other groups didn't want to deal with me or her either. Most didn't return my calls. Rectifying a hoarder or collector situation requires a multifocal, specialized team including veterinarians, rescue organizations, spay/neuter surgery groups, law enforcement, the courts, mental health professionals, and money—lots of it. Of course, it will also involve heartbreaking circumstances. Intervention isn't always successful; recidivism among hoarders is high. I know that now.

With my initial contact with the collector a failure, her daughter suggested I come to the property to see the situation firsthand at a time when her mother would be gone for a few hours. I drove there the next morning. Opening the car door, I involuntarily held my breath as the noxious ammonia odor of urine stung my eyes and nose. At 10:00 am the temperature was already 85-degrees, the air unstirring with the rank stench. To my left an eight-foot tangled towering tunnel of trash and debris funneled visitors to a rusty pink trailer's door. The woman's daughter, a short heavy-set young woman of about 20, approached me. With a cigarette dangling from her lips, she nodded and pointed a stubby finger to my right. I turned and counted fifteen cats in a chicken-wire cage which was fastened to wood stakes stuck in the dirt. The cats were in the shade, but that was the only thing right about this. Cloudy green water fermented in dirty pails on the ground. Torn soggy paper food bowls littered the pen. Thin, dirty, and dull-coated, most of the cats sat scratching and licking, and I could see runny, crusty eyes. As I approached their pen, the cats moved forward in a wave in hopes I had food. Some put front legs up on the thin wire, stretching to reach a frantically grasping paw through to me.

Next to the pen stood a weather-beaten rusted tin shed, about six-feet tall and three-feet square. A corroded padlock secured a stained metal corrugated door. I could hear cats mewing inside. I jiggled and yanked at the lock, beat on it, pulled on it. I couldn't get past it.

Appalled at what I saw and stymied at releasing the shed cats, I shot fast photographs of the cats I could see. I left with a headache from the ammonia fumes, but not before my car's rear wheels sank into the muddy drive and I had to rock it back and forth to extricate it.

At home, I first contacted that county's Sheriff. No help. No time for cats. Via the internet I found an animal-friendly lawyer in southern Mississippi. He agreed to help, at least with letter writing and legal guidance, pro bono. Another few calls and I had the name of a Deputy Sheriff who reportedly had a soft spot for animals. Calling him, I described the situation and pleaded that he intervene and stop the suffering that day. He agreed to visit. The next morning he called me. He'd been out and talked to the collector, giving her two weeks to get the situation cleaned up. Dismayed and disappointed, I dropped my head into my hands and groaned. It meant all of the cats would suffer at least two more weeks. I inquired about the condition of the cats locked in the shed. He hadn't seen them, having not asked the owner to unlock the shed. He explained that the smell was overwhelming and he wanted to leave. He'd just instructed her to call me.

I didn't fully understand hoarders at that time, but there wasn't as much research on the disorder available either, and my rural internet access in 1999 was limited. I hoped that an order from the law enforcement officer to "clean up" the situation, coupled with our offer of free veterinary care for all the cats— including allowing her to keep two cats of her choice—would tip this collector's decision to relinquish the remaining animals. I'd recently established a new relationship with a veterinarian in Memphis, and she'd just met with the director of an appealing new cat sanctuary in the area. If I could convince the collector to release the cats, the sanctuary would take them if they underwent spay or neuter surgery first, and they would try to place them.

With this two-week wait in effect, the lawyer mailed a letter to the collector, advising her of State of Mississippi animal cruelty statutes and warning that unless she cooperated, we'd press charges in court. She did not respond to the letter; she ignored my calls.

The Deputy returned two weeks later. He reported that while the offender had picked up some of the feces under the cats and put out some cleaner (relatively speaking) water, the situation was mostly unchanged. I was baffled that he again didn't ask to see the cats in the shed; he said his time was required on other matters. Case closed. Stalemate.

With my other options exhausted, I spoke to the attorney, who explained the process of swearing out a warrant for the woman on animal cruelty charges. In that day, any citizen could do that. I drove to that County's Courthouse the next morning. Entering through the warped and creaking wood doors of the century old historic building, I made my way to the Court Clerk's office and approached the chipped Formica countertop. I announced I wanted to swear out a warrant for another's arrest, and the clerk pushed a form across the counter at me. I printed my allegations. The Clerk reviewed my affidavit, then instructed me to face the American flag, raise my right hand, and attest that this narrative of animal cruelty was factual and true. It's the first, and I hope last time, I will ever swear out a warrant for someone's arrest. It is not a good feeling.

The warrant was served on the woman as she stood in the door of her trailer that night. The Deputies agreed to allow her to remain free at home without being processed through the jail until the court date in two weeks. On that day, I would present my observations to the judge, then the collector would be given an opportunity to refute me. I arranged to take off work to be present for court, but the afternoon before the court date the collector called me and said I could come get the cats. Stunned, relieved, and thrilled the cats would soon be free, I started stuffing crates into the back of my car. I loaded them with my phone pressed between my ear and shoulder as I called the Sheriff's office and requested a Deputy to accompany me for the surrender. The original caller had said her mom and her heavily tattooed brothers were angry with me, and as their trailer was isolated, I had some fear for my safety, especially with nonexistent cellular phone service in that area. The Sheriff's Office initially refused but finally relented, and agreed to provide an escort for me. I drove to meet the Deputy at the Sheriff's headquarters at the county jail. Sitting for an hour warming a worn wood bench, I rubbed elbows with handcuffed jail detainees and endured their smirks while I waited for the Deputy who would accompany me. I suspect that was on purpose. It was an experience I won't forget.

The sun was starting to set as I arrived at the trailer home and unloaded my crates; a beefy Deputy Sheriff clad in polyester khaki and green led the way in his squad car, over dirt backroads and creaky, sagging wood bridges. Once there, he leaned against a tree, flicked the toothpick residing in the corner of his mouth, and chuckled at my cat wrangling techniques as I slipped and slid in the mud, grabbing cats. Fortunately, the cats were socialized and easy to handle. Leaning against the trailer door, barely visible in the shadows of the trash tunnel, the cat collector watched, unblinking. Corkscrew wild untamed dark hair framed a grim, stony face. Deep dark eyes were set hard against me. That ice-cold glare kept me from approaching her, and we never spoke.

With the penned cats crated, the daughter unlocked the shed. Ammonia odor watered my eyes again, the smell so strong it propelled me back two steps. Blurred vision from my watering eyes did help obscure the horrifying images of those cats in the shed. Consisting of nearly two-feet of fecal and organic matter, the elevated foundation supported six cats, huddled together, sides touching in the dark. Easily crated, the frightened cats were loaded into my car, blinking and squinting in the waning light. The Deputy and I departed.

I'd already arranged to transport the 21 cats to an area veterinary clinic for triage and stabilization upon confiscation. It was after 8 pm when I arrived. After a cursory assessment of each cat, I attached notes for the veterinarian, and hung bowls of fresh water in each crate. Instantly a tune of tongues lapping, lapping, lapping filled the room as the cats drained their water bowls before moving to the cans of food I shoved in.

The next morning, the vet examined the cats, all of whom were thin with dull coats, worms, and fleas. No cats had feline leukemia or immunodeficiency virus, but they were malnourished and in poor body condition. One cat had sustained a traumatic eye injury, and she underwent surgery to remove the irreparably damaged eye. But overall, it was reasonably good news, he found little that fresh air and good food wouldn't fix. After he pronounced all healthy enough for transport, another volunteer helped me clean up and load the crated cats. With the back of the car filled with cats, we hauled them to a clinic in another town for spay/neuter surgery. From there the cats traveled on to the new cat sanctuary. All of the cats recovered uneventfully with medical care and proper nutrition.

Shortly after the confiscation, I heard the collector had returned to her Texas family. Ten years later, rumor had it she'd returned to our area and was back to collecting cats. Recidivism is the norm and not the exception in hoarders, most of whom meet criteria for mental illness. I know now that hoarding behaviors are baffling, bizarre, egregious, and refractory to treatment.

I am glad I liberated those cats from that situation. I treasure the memory of those tiny tongues lapping up fresh water, refreshing their fluid volumes and quenching their thirst.

I learned though that animal hoarders need intensive intervention, far more than *any* one person or organization can offer. This multifaceted intervention will require a tremendous investment of resources, especially money. The time I spent liberating the cats from the collector impacted my personal and professional life: Try telling your employer you need time off for court. They don't like it. And be prepared to be consumed with most hoarding cases for months and more. This was a small hoarding case, but some collectors will acquire cats or dogs numbering in the hundreds. While admitting cats to this new sanctuary was rewarding at the time, I visited eight months later to find that same sanctuary near failure, the number of cats burgeoning, and the operators admitting they were living on credit cards. The number of cats needing shelter had within a matter of months outstripped their ability to provide it. It's not surprising that legitimate nonprofits fail and themselves become the subject of cruelty investigations; they can become overwhelmed with animals and underwhelmed with funds and helpers.

Finally, I regret initially turning over the situation to the Deputy Sheriff. Once he'd given the woman a two-week reprieve, he'd effectively sentenced the cats to more suffering in the cage and shed, and I could find nothing I could do about it. Be careful to whom you surrender control. If I did face this type situation again and chose to become involved, I would never go it alone. I would muster an alliance of professionals and insist we go forward united, with the might and strength of multiple organizations and resources behind us. I'd make sure we had a team who could push past a blockade and help the suffering animals. Networking via the internet should make that more likely a reality now.

I learned from this that an animal hoarding situation is a heartrending tragedy which cannot be managed by one person. You're gonna need help.

These cats are recovering after spay/neuter surgeries in our spay/ neuter surgery unit, which is a used travel trailer we converted into a surgical facility. The clear plastic bubble wrap helps keep them warm, although they are also on heating pads set at 100-degrees. A nurse, who has stepped aside for the photo, is continually present to monitor their condition. Once recovering cats begin to lift their heads, we return them to their crates, but close observation continues until discharge later the same day. Hand sanitizer is used between cats to reduce disease transmission. Corn syrup is rubbed on gums to increase blood glucose if needed. Tattoo ink (green in this case) is applied beside the spay incision to identify it as such, rather than another type of abdominal surgery—if the cat doesn't get its left ear tipped. Each cat has paperwork consisting of owner permission for surgery, along with the cat's medical and surgical record. It includes the medications administered and the treatments applied. Neckbands serve as identification; fractious and feral cats have their neckband removed and wrapped around a paw before they awaken.

CHAPTER 13

No Deal

The vet is out

SEATED WITH MY cat near the receptionist in the veterinarian's waiting room, I studied the bedraggled appearance of the stooped, boney, elderly woman who stepped in from the sweltering July heat. Wearing a cotton summer dress worn so threadbare it was almost translucent, she stopped and swiped a wadded tissue across her sweating brow. Knee-high hose with holes sagged at her ankles. The soles of her disintegrating shoes pulled away from the uppers. Wiping damp gray hair away out of her eyes, she approached the receptionist and laid three crumpled one-dollar bills on the counter. She requested three birth control pills for her cats. The receptionist in turn handed her a tiny manila Rx envelope; the woman slid the packet into her pocket, nodded at those of us waiting, and departed.

"Birth control pills for cats?" I asked, as the door closed. "I've never heard of that."

"No surprise, because it usually doesn't work. It's a hormone that affects the cat's heat cycles. That lady walks I don't know how many miles here to get those pills, trying to keep her cats from getting pregnant. She's been doing that as long as I've been here, that's five years. Says she doesn't have a car."

Seeing this woman, aged and worn, counting out three one-dollar bills to try to keep her cats from littering, washed sadness over me. How blessed I was: There I sat in the air-conditioned room, wearing fresh neat clothing, with my car parked outside, and my money for my cat's care in my pocket. I silently gave thanks for my job and my many blessings, then made a snap decision to offer these three cats the gift of spays. It was an impulse buy, my treat for these obviously loved cats.

Mind made up, when I was called into the exam room with my cat, I shut the door behind me and pulled out my VISA. I slid it across the exam table to the vet.

"That lady that was just in here? I'll pay for her three cat spays," I said.

"No," said the vet, pushing the credit card back at me.

"Why?" I asked, puzzled.

"Because she'll go tell everyone she got a free spay here at my clinic," he replied.

"Tell her it *wasn't* free, that someone else paid for it," I countered. Baffled and bewildered that he was turning down my full, undiscounted payment to improve the health of three cats and reduce the monumental overpopulation of suffering cats in our county, I pushed the blue plastic credit card back across the exam table again.

"No," he repeated, elevating his chin, setting his jaw, and crossing his arms over his chest, the overhead light reflecting off his glasses. "What you gotta understand is that lady could have paid for a spay already with the money she's been spending each month for years now on those pills."

"What you gotta understand is this woman will never have $90 at one time to get a cat fixed! She's poor!" I retorted, feeling anger rising.

But the vet wouldn't budge, and I left floundering in frustration. I never utilized his veterinary clinic again. I will not support an animal doctor who refuses to accept full payment for the care of an elderly indigent woman's pets. I never did discover the woman's identity so I could help her cats directly.

You might be thinking: "She shouldn't have cats if she can't afford to take care of them." But low-income folks do have pets. They enjoy their company just as you and I do. They haven't been blessed with the resources to care for them. The overwhelming majority of pet owners we serve never sought out a pet, never answered an ad for a free or pricey pet, and certainly never entered a pet store. They were only kind enough to share their food and shelter when a homeless cat or dog showed up, rather than shoot it or poison it. Like urban areas, rural communities are populated with the poor, and small towns can rarely offer services on par with those available in urban areas—think humane societies and shelters where one could surrender a stray, or low-cost spay/neuter surgeries, or even veterinary care clinics.

We have clients drive from counties in rural Mississippi that have no veterinary clinic; pet owners have driven more than 100 miles one direction to get their cat to us, waiting in the car all day in the heat or the cold, all to get the cat neutered. Those are the people who have a car that can make it that distance, is legal for the road, and who can save enough money, or borrow it, for the fuel. People without cars or cash can't make that choice.

The lesson I learned here is to unfailingly reflect upon and give thanks for my bounty of blessings. I give thanks for people who care enough to walk dusty hot roads to get a pill for a cat to try to stop her litter. I give thanks for people who will give up their whole day and drive for hours to get a pet fixed. Finally, I learned to put my money where my mouth is when spending for my pets' care. Veterinarians are entitled to run their practices to meet their financial needs. And I am entitled to hand my money to professionals whose values and ethics reflect mine. I encourage you to do the same.

Veterinarians and euthanasia technicians do not "put animals to sleep." Euthanasia is the correct term for the humane and elective ending of an animal's life. In animal welfare discourse, my opinion is we should avoid substituting "put to sleep" for "euthanasia." Unless you can wake up the cat or dog you've just "put to sleep," it certainly isn't accurate. "Put to sleep" is a family-friendly euphemism that keeps people from being too uncomfortable with what's really happening, but it is not a factual or truthful description. Maybe it makes us feel better to say "put to sleep" rather than "euthanize" an animal, but I support using the actual term "euthanasia" to refer to ending an animal's life. It is the correct term to use in describing the procedure whether it makes others uncomfortable or not.

CHAPTER 14

Grandma

Poverty and priorities

WE WENT TO evaluate a report of an elderly man who needed help with his cats. On our return on a rural road, we spotted dogs chained a short distance behind a dilapidated little house of about 700 square feet. The word *house* here is an inadequate portrayal of a structure that could hardly be described as that. Pulling in the dusty dirt drive, we got a closer view of the four beefy black dogs, who appeared to be Pit Bulls. Each on the end of heavy chains, the dogs stared dully at us. Only one barked, and he didn't go to much trouble. No tails wagged. The other volunteer headed toward the dogs; I tapped on the open door of the structure and it swung open with a creak. I stepped inside, calling "hello?"

On the floor, supine on the soiled, deflated, flattened remains of a mattress, was an obese elderly woman, her advanced age confirmed by her appearance. Beside her was a ceramic bowl used as a chamber pot. Full. In 2004. A solitary chair stood in the corner. On the opposite corner there was a sink and an old refrigerator, apparently non-functional. A few torn, stained curtains fluttered at the broken windows as the afternoon sun streamed in.

"Hi honey," said the woman, smiling up at me from the floor. "How are you?"

"Uh, hello," I muttered, trying to squelch my expression of staggering stupefaction. Was I in the United States of America?

"Um, we saw your dogs. We're offering free rabies shots and free animal birth control surgery for dogs and cats," I muttered.

Standing in that one-room shack, with a bed-ridden elderly woman lying not in a bed but on the floor on a stained mattress with her excrement in a bowl beside her, I cannot even begin to describe how petty, how inane, how tiny, how insignificant I felt for announcing why I'd come: To help the *dogs*.

"Those are my grandson's dogs," she replied, still smiling, eyes friendly. "You'd need to talk to him."

She had such a sweet smile, but I couldn't return it. I just stood there dumbfounded.

Hearing a truck pull into the drive snapped me back to reality. I turned to the open door. A strapping young man hopped out of a rattletrap truck. He froze when he saw me.

"Hello," I said, trying to seem confident now by throwing my hand up in a friendly wave. I still couldn't get a smile on my face to match it though. "We're offering free animal birth control surgery for dogs today, and we saw yours."

"Those are high blood dogs," he said, still unmoving. His cold dark eyes met mine. "You wouldn't ever wanna cut 'em. Besides, I gotta lotta money in those dogs."

I lost it. An old woman on a stinking mattress. A pot of you know what beside her. Miserable dogs on chains. A shack.

"You've got a lot of money tied up in dogs while your grandmother lies on the floor on a rotting mattress with her own filth beside her? You have money in dogs but that's your own grandmother in that stinking house?" I exclaimed.

Without realizing it I stormed at him with my hands balled into fists and my jaw clenched. As I closed the distance though, I heard my colleague returning from checking the dogs, and my rational brain reignited: Stop it. Back away. Leave. Now. There are few women who will win a fight with a man. I am not one of them. We turned away and departed.

From this experience, I learned that to accomplish your mission, you have to stay focused. Where you find animals suffering, you will find people suffering too. These predicaments are bonded and joined.

After this I lost my focus for a while: I delivered groceries, called child welfare services and law enforcement for suspected abuse, had locks changed on the door of elderly pet owner who'd been raped by a neighbor, arranged cataract surgery and the transportation to it for an old man after we fixed his dog and cat. Aiding those in despair limited my ability to help suffering animals though.

You will face the same ethical issues if you intervene to help less fortunate animals. Competing needs will draw you in different directions. Which will take priority? Write down what you want to do to reduce suffering—animal or human—then list the steady, individual, manageable steps necessary to achieve those goals. Dream big; start small. Budget your time. Unless you are independently wealthy and live alone with no other responsibilities, pace yourself. Otherwise your health may fail, your family will feel abandoned, and you risk becoming immobilized by the overwhelming sorrow of the condition of our planet, its creatures, its people. Decide now where you will direct your efforts.

We were once asked by an elderly woman to help fix her 12 cats. Because she said she didn't have transportation, we traveled to her home in an secluded rural area. After we assessed her outdoor cats, she invited us to see her two housecats. Stepping into her home, we were astonished to see four walls of one room literally papered with certificates of appreciation from a major animal welfare organization, thanking her for the donations. Stuck up with cellophane tape, the papers covered every inch of every wall in the room. We stood slack-jawed, staring.

"I give to them," she announced proudly. "I love animals."

I suggested she keep her money for use on her own animals. She had met our low-income requirements, and had called us because she said she couldn't afford to fix her pets.

"But they have those ads on tv, and it is so sad, and I want to help," she replied.

Repeating that if she had animals in need of care, I advised she spend her money on those animals, rather than mailing funds off to a big city group, then calling the small local charity to help.

"But I thought when I gave, it came to you," she said, looking dismayed.

Animal welfare organizations are not all linked. We are separate entities. Giving money to a major national organization doesn't mean that group will simply send it on to a smaller local group.

She's neither the first nor the last person we met who believed this. If you give, give local.

Elderly woman (purple robe near cat) with her cat (circled) and dog that we fixed

CHAPTER 15

Down Dog

Mississippi microchip

SOON AFTER WE moved to northern Mississippi, I glimpsed through tall, overgrown green grass the heads of two large short-hair golden–red dogs. Spotting them about one mile from my house, I passed them before dawn on the narrow blacktop road on my way to work. I couldn't stop then, but I searched for them that afternoon. Two boisterous, lean, friendly females bounded to me as I called. I placed a bowl of food in front of them. It was licked clean in twenty seconds. Stroking their pretty heads, I lifted their lips, saw no tartar on the shiny white teeth. Young, maybe a year-old? I walked to the nearest home and asked the homeowner if he knew anything about the dogs. No, he didn't, and if they approached his cattle, he would shoot them. That cruelty is known as a Mississippi Microchip—buckshot in the groin and butt as a dog flees. And if they didn't move on in a few days, he planned to load them into his pickup truck bed, drive them five miles down the road, and push them out to be someone else's problem. In his experience he explained, five miles is the minimum dump distance required to avoid them returning. A common solution.

Returning to the dogs, I herded them both onto my car's backseat. I drove the friendly bouncing balls of energy to my home and confined them in our outdoor sheltered kennel, where they pawed, dug, jumped, whined, and barked most of the night. Believing all dogs to be good dogs though, I cheerfully peddled the canines at work the next day, showing off photos through the new wonder of digital photography, describing their lighthearted energetic personalities, and depicting their beauty. The cleaning lady, who'd never had a pet in her life, said she'd like one.

"Gonna get me a dog!" she crowed, and I beamed, so pleased to have placed the dog. The next morning, I crated both dogs for the drive to the veterinarian for their spay surgeries. The vet was to give the adopter a basic dog care booklet and new dog kit when she picked up her new dog that afternoon. I drove the other still nonstop bouncing spinning canine home with me later that day. Surgery and anesthesia hadn't stunted that energetic dog even for a minute.

As I opened the door of the crate in the backseat, the dog burst through and leaped from the car, tearing the leash from my hand and nearly flattening me in the process. Leather lead flapping behind her, she sped down the driveway to the road. I raced after her but I can still to this day hear the sound of a speeding truck, the screech of brakes, and a sickening thud. The dog was dead. That quick. Heartbroken, I sank even deeper into remorse and regret two days later when the adopter informed me she'd returned her dog to the vet's clinic.

"That dog runnin' all over the place, jumpin' on the furniture, barkin' all the time, knockin' things over, tearin' stuff up, racin' out the door. I gotta chase her everywhere. I gotta clean up after her. I can't deal with that," she said.

The vet was annoyed too.

"These are animals, not toys, and this isn't a game where you take one home and then decide you don't want to fool with it," he huffed, justifiably critical of my dim-witted, ill-considered decision to place the dog in this home.

I'd been taught a sad and sobering lesson. I'm glad it smacked some sense into me early. I had been naïve. Pondering how I failed both dogs, I believe I thought love would trump any issues these dogs had. Overlooking reality and oversimplifying, I assumed an almost child-like belief that most people have a tender spot in their heart for a dog. I believed they'd have or acquire the patience and the skills needed to transform a homeless disadvantaged dog into a treasured family pet. I admit that at that time, I had never attempted it myself.

Seldom handled as pups, young dogs who stray away from rural farm communities and low-income homes to wander once they are sexually mature can be challenging pets. They've never been taught any manners; they've never even been in a house. They're brimming with energy. Because they've been living outdoors, their prey instinct may be fine-tuned to chase anything from livestock to wildlife to other pets. They'll chew up a two-week old deer carcass outdoors then puke up that bucket-load up on your slippers just after you tuck into bed for the night.

I have learned too that most people want a pet, not a project. When the decision is made to get a dog, people often search for what they want when they want it, and a responsible adopter doesn't usually make a snap decision on the spot. They've already considered their circumstances and determined what they can reasonably manage in a dog or cat before they begin the search for the right one.

Make no mistake: Stray and free-roaming dogs can and should be screened and given an opportunity for a behavioral assessment and possible rehoming. And all adopters should be screened for what they will and won't tolerate in a dog before being offered one. A few dogs are going to require ongoing training, some even over their lifetime, in order to be maintained as pets—witness the plethora of dog trainers, books, blogs, websites, training devices, and reality TV shows about difficult dogs who bite, bark, destroy, attack, jump, and chase. All that zipped right over my head and I am fortunate that there were no disasters, such as biting a child or attacking someone, while the surviving dog was in this inexperienced adopter's custody. The vet eventually placed the remaining dog in a farm home, where she could run for hours every day, and for that I am grateful. In the years that followed, I offered a few homeless dogs for adoption, typically only small dogs. That was only after an adoption assessment, personality test, and trial of home manners. Now there are a multitude of dog rescues with staff imminently more qualified than me to assess and place dogs, and I let them do it.

Shooting small animals as a method of population control is ineffective, even before you consider the inherent cruelty. Because they are nimble and athletic, dogs and cats are most often wounded in the hindquarters as they flee, rather than being instantly killed. The result is crippling injuries like shattered hind legs or a fractured pelvis. Shooting increases the suffering. There are humane alternatives and most jurisdictions have laws to back that up. Use them to go after these perpetrators.

CHAPTER 16

Diamond

Water water everywhere

OUR ORGANIZATION BELIEVED upcoming veterinary students could benefit from seeing real-life scenarios of pets in rural Mississippi, especially impoverished areas. Many animals treated by veterinary students at the college are beloved pets of owners who will spend almost any amount and sacrifice significant slices of their life for them. We wanted to expose students to the difficulties that pet owners on the other side of the income divide face in providing proper care.

For example, we encountered a dog whose owner complained that the animal was often constipated. In addition to recommending a premium, expensive dog food not found within 50-miles of this trailer, the senior vet student explained to the owner that canned pumpkin is helpful with constipation. But this family lived 12 miles from a grocery that sold canned pumpkin, and they owned no car. In addition, we stood on a frayed orange extension cord that ran from the opposite trailer, powering a fan inside this trailer—the only electrical appliance running in there. There were no funds for even a can of pumpkin.

Veterinary students, one holding the dog, talk with the owner

Other issues arise too when you peruse neighborhoods looking for animals in need. Trespassing, interfering, and just plain not minding your own business is how the community may perceive your efforts.

One Saturday, I took four senior veterinary medicine students to an indigent neighborhood just outside a tiny resource-barren town of 900. Spotting a dog chained to a pine tree behind an algae-stained clapboard house, we pulled over and parked. You and I buy security systems for our homes; low-income homeowners chain up a big dog out back.

Ears alert, the pretty blonde dog stood and wagged at our approach, her hips swaying happily. Panting in the July heat, the Lab-type mix had no water. I found an empty Folgers coffee can in the detritus around the house, and as I searched for a spigot, I heard a door squeak open behind me. I turned to face hostile heavy eyes set high in the face of a gargantuan-sized woman. She wore a thin cotton housedress patterned with pastel pink flowers, totally incongruous with her stature and her glare.

"What are you doing?" she snapped, hands on hips, from the top of grease-stained preformed concrete steps.

"Hello," I said. "Your dog has no water. I'm just getting her some."

"That dog has water," she retorted.

Looking around me, I saw none.

"I don't see any. I'll just get her some."

"That dog has water," she snapped.

Confused, I rotated 360-degrees again, looking for the water. I saw no water other than that in my hand.

"That dog has water," she repeated stubbornly, defying reality. "The dog has water."

After a brief and tense conversation, the irritable giant reluctantly agreed to let me fill a bowl with water for the dog. She also consented to having the dog spayed; the mention that a free state-required rabies tag would be issued facilitated that agreement. I would have to do the transporting. We left the dog with a full bowl of water, and the owner's consent to let me fetch Diamond two days later. After spay and vaccination, sweet Diamond was returned to her chained existence. Pounding a wood tomato plant stake into the baked earth, I slid an old Bundt-type cake pan with a hole in the center over the stake so Diamond couldn't knock over the pan, and I filled it with water. I left an ant-proof container filled with 20 pounds of dog food at their back door, along with a scoop and a bowl for Diamond. In her absence the family had erected a wading pool, about 3-feet deep and 8-feet around. Filled with sparkling fresh water, it was cruelly placed one foot out of Diamond's reach. That irony wasn't lost on anyone but the owner.

If you're thinking, "I wouldn't have returned her," decide first what you're going to do with a poorly socialized dog who's spent her life on a chain with little positive human interaction. You can't just place her as a family pet because she'll need professional help first, probably a lot. Few homes exist anyway. You could make a persuasive argument that euthanasia is kinder, but the owner didn't and wouldn't consent to that. Maybe you'd decide to slip by sometime and release the dog from her chain, or steal her. Then you could face criminal charges; animal rescuers have been successfully criminally prosecuted for taking animals they considered to be abused or neglected, plus you would still need to place the dog in a home. And finally, you take this dog off the chain, they'll fasten another to that chain in a matter of days: a dog from the side of the road, one somebody doesn't want, one of the free puppies in a box at the Dollar General store, or a tired mama dog left tied in the Walmart parking lot.

Encouraging the owners to bring a dog into the house isn't a viable option either for people who barely have enough room for themselves in the house, or for people who have for generations understood that animals live outdoors. Or for people who never wanted a pet, only a watchdog. You and I see treasure, some see pests. Even if this family had opened their door to Diamond, neither they nor the majority of us have the skills to train a dog in obedience and house manners. Fewer than that know how to transform previously chained dogs into well-behaved house pets. A fenced kennel donated and erected by volunteers might be welcomed, and it might be at the local pawn shop a few hours later too.

Diamond later broke free of her chain and vanished. I stopped by to retrieve the dog food container I'd delivered four months earlier, but left seething and heartsick when I found it untouched, still filled to the brim with now moldy dog food. A few months later that family departed and the home was condemned.

From Diamond I learned that I am blessed to have running water, a roof over my head, and the patience to speak the truth to a defensive owner's gaslighting. I also learned from Diamond the realities of life for dogs on chains, and the grim fact that there are no easy answers for these dogs. Our work here is nowhere near finished, and I give thanks for those who are toiling to free dogs from lives on chains.

Harvest wisdom from animals. Learn from them. Observe their rhythms of daily living; watch them rest, eat, play, groom, sleep. Study their cycles of life: hunkering down in winter, frolicking in spring, grazing through summer, then stocking, storing, and prepping in autumn for the lean winter on their horizons.

But ask the beasts, and they will teach you;
Ask the birds of the air to inform you,
Or tell the creatures that crawl to teach you,
and the fish of the sea to instruct you...
Job 12:7-8, Revised English Bible

Ginger

CHAPTER 17

Ginger

Cat in a box

WHEN A MAN from an auto repair business called one day to report he had an injured cat, I advised him to get her to a vet.

"She's not our cat. She hangs around here. We've been feeding her, but we don't have anyone who can leave and drive her to a vet, and besides, none of us can pay for that," he said. "She's not real friendly and she's hurt pretty bad. We found her hanging by her leg from a piece of equipment. That whole leg is tore up. She's all bloody from trying to get loose. We fed her Saturday afternoon, but Sunday she didn't come to eat, and then this morning when we opened up the shop, we saw her hanging by her back leg from a machine back there in the garage. Figure she probably got hung up sometime after we left on Saturday, and that's why she didn't come to eat Sunday. Guys got all torn up getting her loose. We got her in a box now."

While we don't operate as a rescue, this tale motivates any animal lover, so I alerted the vet of incoming casualty and drove to the business. Unrushed, the guy finished with his customer as I fretted and fidgeted. Finally bending behind the counter, he resurfaced with a tattered cardboard box and pushed it across the dingy counter to me. I peered between the flaps at a slender, orange-and-white short-hair cat. She didn't move, but I could see her breathing and I could see blood. Clutching the box under one arm and pressing the top shut with the other, I left with her.

"Nerve damage," the vet said as he pulled the depressed and frightened cat from the box. He proved it by squeezing the paw of the damaged hind leg. No reaction from the cat. "I don't think that leg can be saved."

He admitted her to ICU and splinted then bandaged the leg, and started antibiotics. The cat had lacerated her skin and fractured her ankle as she struggled to free her leg. Because the skin had shredded in the battle, there was simply nothing to stitch shut. Those wounds would have to heal from the inside out, and required frequent re-dressing.

Gradually, the cat perked up. About a year old and not well socialized, I marvel now at how she maintained her calm through that ordeal. Cringing at the thought of the pain she must have endured, I wonder to this day how she ever found the strength to purr again. Anyone who's spent any time with sick or injured dogs and cats knows that sometimes those animals seem to understand we are helping them, and they do try sometimes to cooperate. When efforts to save the irreparably damaged leg proved futile, the decision was made to amputate at the time of her spay. Sailing through that and now named Ginger, she came home to be my house pet, as handicapped cats are not candidates for outdoor living. We also trapped her two kittens in the junkyard behind the business, and after sterilization they were placed in adoptive homes.

My heart broke again after Ginger developed a nasal cancer when she was about 5 years old, and she was subsequently euthanized when the battle was lost. While her life was short, it was so sweet and I treasured the time I had with her. The lesson I learned, by remembering her stunning beauty and quiet good cheer, is that there is no benefit to bitterness when one survives grievous injury only to be struck down by a terminal illness. Bitterness will eat you up: The beast at that feast is you. None of us knows our date of departure. We can only give thanks for our pets and friends right now, then delight in the day we are living, right this minute, with these exquisite creatures sharing our planet.

Thinking back to those burly, tattooed, tobacco-spitting men who helped her, I learned too that kindness can be found in places where you least expect it. When those men found a terrified, bloody, struggling cat dangling by a hind leg, they could have chosen to end her dilemma in another way, one that wouldn't have involved them being bitten and scratched while trying to free her. They didn't do that. They chose kindness and two guys got hurt helping her. But then they called us to help this magnificent and elegant homeless cat before dressing their own wounds. They gave Ginger her life and they gave me hope. You gotta love that.

Veterinary students canvass a low-income neighborhood for pets needing spay/neuter

Starting 20 years ago, the Homeless Animals Relief Project helped train veterinary students in the early-age spay/neuter surgery of puppies and kittens. The skill is now routinely taught in their training, because it's been proven safe for the pet and effective in reducing animal overpopulation. In this photo veterinary medicine students canvass a neighborhood for pets in need of birth control surgery. Failure to stop a litter in rural or less fortunate areas often results in emaciated, diseased, and malnourished wormy kittens with crusted, runny eyes. Frightened, boney mother cats slink around in the shadows; battered tomcats with torn ears, swollen slashed faces, and bite-wound abscesses stalk them and rival males. It does not need to be this way. Early-age spay/neuter surgery is tried and true. Repeatedly proven safe, it halts the killing, the unwanted litters, and the obstetric nightmare of babies having babies.

Patches

CHAPTER 18

Patches

Advocates always ask

IN EARLY 1997, as I worked to get pets fixed one by one, I got a call from a low-income family in a nearby rural small town. They had a cat named Patches, and they couldn't afford the cost of spay surgery. When I asked the cat's age, the owner said he thought she was five, and that she'd had 12 litters. I expressed surprise, but he assured me that was correct.

"One time they [the kittens] came early, and they all died, but all the other litters were fine. She never had less than six at a time, except that one time she lost them, and that time there was eight of them," he said.

He met me with Patches a week later so I could drive her on to her appointment for surgery; he handed me a wire cage tied together with baling twine. Inside I saw a cat who with a useless front leg. The paw bent back and up onto the leg in a permanent contracture. The joint where the lower leg met the paw was worn through. Dry dirty bone was visible where the cat's coat had worn away.

"What happened here?" I queried, as he hadn't mentioned the crippling injury when we talked.

"Been like that for years," he replied. "Don't know what happened. Came home dragging that leg one day."

At the clinic the veterinarian watched the calico short-hair cat ambulate. To walk she hopped with her back legs and dragged the front leg; a faster pace required her to swing the leg forward, bear weight on the exposed joint surface, and lean in for the next stride. The constant pressure on the joint's surface broke down the skin and tissue, exposing this bare bone. She exhibited no tenderness there though. Often caused by a collision with a car, a brachial plexus injury can sever or damage the nerve supplying the front leg, making it impossible for the animal to move naturally and deadening the limb to pain. Recommending an amputation of the useless leg, the vet said she'd be fine without the limb, but he fiercely advocated a permanent indoor home.

I called the owner. No surprise, he couldn't pay for an amputation, and no, he would not agree to keep the cat indoors even if we covered the cost. He surrendered the cat to us, and I fell in love with this gentle, gracious creature. After the amputation in 1997, she was discharged home to me with some pain pills. Have you ever wrestled a fresh amputee to stuff a chunky pill down her throat? It only terrified her, so she went through the recovery with only rest and heat. Soft and fluffy, cheerful and steady, she graced our home and enriched our lives for another ten years. Missing a front limb never fazed her. She did get clumsy at times when jumping up on furniture, and I applied colorful claw covers to her remaining front nails to protect fabrics.

From Patches I learned to always ask owners about their pet's general health when I schedule them for surgery—duh! I also realized I had to better advocate for animals in my care who are experiencing pain. It was about a decade later before pain relief for animals came to the forefront of veterinary medicine. Now pets may go home from this type of major surgery with an extended release pain patch stitched to their shaved skin, or at the very least with a pack of tiny tasty, chewable pain pills. Neither was offered to Patches in 1997. I do wish that when I couldn't get the pills down her I had lobbied for injectable or maybe liquid pain medication I could give her, or even returned her to the clinic for pain management. When your charges have surgery, ask how their pain will be managed, because animals feel pain just like you and I. This is a scientific, undisputed fact.

Multitudes of vets are still advising "wait until they are six months old" for spay/neuter. We recognize now that by then most cats will be pregnant, and a few will have already delivered their first litter. I testify to this because I have witnessed it. Tiny cats, some appearing less than 18-20 weeks old and weighing only around four pounds, come in with the telltale rotund belly of pregnancy. It is pitiful, it is sad, it is grievous, and it is heartbreaking. These mothers are little more than kittens themselves, and they've been deprived of their youth. Some will be deprived of their life by their juvenile pregnancy. Nutrition that should be strengthening the heart, brain, and bones is rationed for the lives within the uterus; both mother and fetuses will suffer. Fix by five.

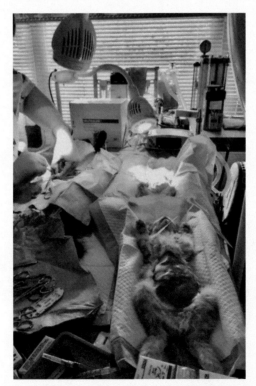

Anesthetized cats awaiting surgery in our spay/neuter trailer

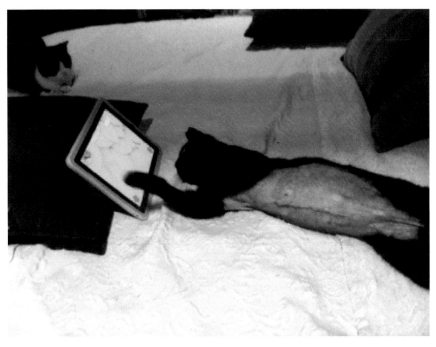

Charles resting as ordered after surgery, he is playing a cat game on the tablet

CHAPTER 19

Charles

Better breathing

SOME WEEKENDS WITH nice weather, when people will be out in their yards, we cruise low-income areas recruiting dogs and cats for spay/neuter surgery. A lot of community residents don't know what spay/neuter surgery is, wouldn't consider it if they did because of cost, and don't have a car to transport the dog or cat to a vet clinic that is miles away. If they do have a car, they won't allow the animal in the car for fear of soiling, and they don't have a carrier for a pet. These neighborhood residents frankly seem to have problems they consider far more important than whether or not the dog or cat is fixed. Looking around, you would be hard pressed to disagree. But we hand out our cards or informational fliers, chat with residents wherever we see pets, and offer a free fix. Knowing that if we don't take the animal when we secure consent to spay/neuter surgery it likely won't get done, we try to crate and transport the dog or cat on the spot if the owner agrees. We house the pet overnight then beg our vet to work them in. We pick up the animal after surgery, care for him or her through recovery, and return the pet to the home later. But considering the payoff received from fixing a pet—the astonishing number of lives that one surgery saved, to say nothing of the dog or cat's health and comfort—it is always worth it.

On one such tour we halted at a four-way-stop, where the volunteer with me spotted a black cat traipsing across the parking lot at a liquor store/gas station. Wheeling in, I stepped from the car, and called. The dull-coated short-hair male cat stopped, eyed me, then kept strolling away. I pulled a cat trap from the back of the car, and within minutes we had captured him. Neutered and vaccinated a few days later, he turned out to be a friendly cat—well social-ized—albeit thin. Unwilling to return him to a location where no one claimed responsibility for his life or his care, I tried to place him, unsuccessfully of course. Black dogs and cats are harder to place than colorful pets; their features aren't often clear in adoption photos, some people are still superstitious about black cats, and adopters are just naturally attracted to unusual colors or mark-ings. It's hard for a black dog to compete with an odd-eyed dog, and a black cat seldom wins the adoption lottery against unusual coat patterns, pretty seal point markings, or blue eyes.

So, this cat became a barn cat at my home. Named Charles—street name Smoke—he ran and ate and played with the other cats. But we soon realized he had a problem: Rapid and shallow breathing was his norm. He breathed about 60-80 times a minute, and his ribcage sucked in hard with each inhalation. He seemed unfazed by it though, and never fell behind the others in play. Nearly a mile from our barn on horseback on the cat's first day with us, I looked back to find Charles trailing along behind me. How he got enough air in his lungs to do that we'll never know, because our trip to the vet yielded a diagnosis of diaphragmatic hernia.

Trauma, probably being hit by a car, tore a hole in his diaphragm—the large sheet-like muscle that separates the lungs from the abdominal contents. The x-ray revealed his intestines, filled with digesting cat food, were coiled up in his chest cavity. With these parts of his intestines squeezed tight into the thorax, Charles' lungs had only limited space to expand for his breathing. No wonder the cat found breathing difficult with both his abdominal contents and lungs stuffed into his chest cavity.

Surgery to repair this is straightforward but not simple: Opening the abdomen for the repair will allow outside air to flow through the hole in the diaphragm and fill the thorax, further compressing the lungs. The surgical team prepares for this by placing a breathing tube when anesthesia is induced and before the incision is made. With that tube in place, the lungs can be inflated with supplemental oxygen to avoid collapse when the abdomen is opened. A long incision is made from the chest to the pelvis to expose the diaphragm. When the hole in the diaphragm is successfully repaired, the breathing tube may be removed. The outside air that has invaded the chest cavity because of the original hole in the diaphragm is gradually sucked out with chest tubes. It's a relatively big operation, and I took Charles to our state veterinary college for the surgery. Thanks to some kindness there for a rescued cat like Charles, the cost was doable.

Should I have donated that money for spay/neuter surgeries for pets living with the poor? Of course. I would have saved dozens of animals instead of one. But when a cat with a personality like Charles' jumps into your arms, huffing and puffing to breathe while flaunting his moxie and lust for life, it's hard to say no. I was blessed to be able to pick up extra work hours to pay for his surgery, and I do not regret it.

From Charles I learned that while I preach sinking our resources into reducing animal overpopulation through spay/neuter surgery, one must acknowledge a special animal, one that speaks to you and says, *Skip the new sofa, buy me an operation instead. How about it?* And you do it for that creature, just as the veterinarians who helped Charles did, in order for a cat to live out the life he has been given. Years later this shiny black cat still sashays up to me, weaves around my ankles and purrs, and it is all worth it.

Navigate to YouTube and search "homeless animals cat with diaphragmatic hernia" to see a video of Charles' breathing before his surgery.

*Juvenile cats anesthetized and prepped for spay. They are
on warming pads and are under a heat lamp.*

*Over the years, we've had cats come in for surgery who are already
in heat, although their owners report them to be just 14 to 16
weeks of age and an exam confirms that. What a relief to get them
in early! They are playing and pouncing in preop, go down for
surgery, and pop right back up in recovery, unlike the older cats
who are worn and frayed from repeated heat/litter cycles. It is
so much easier on cats to be fixed early: There is less blood loss,
and recovery is almost always without complications, unlike with
adult cats. We love it.*

CHAPTER 20

Public Spaces

Not my cat

CRUISING A LOW-INCOME neighborhood, I saw a heavily pregnant, dull-coated, thin white-and-black cat sitting on a front stoop of a crumbling rental home in a public-housing complex. Parking, I approached the elderly gentleman sitting on the porch. With cloudy, milky eyes, he stared suspiciously in my direction. Giving him my card, I explained HARP offered free animal birth control surgery, and I asked if I could take the cat for spay. She circled my ankles as we talked, and I bent forward to finger her coarse coat. Her glorious green eyes met mine and she began to purr.

"I don't know," he said. "That's not my cat. That's my daughter's cat."

I asked to speak to his daughter; he hadn't seen her for months. I asked for her phone number; he didn't have it. I asked when he expected her return; he didn't know. Ending our conversation, he leaned back in his chair, rolled a cigarette, and looked away.

Returning to my car, I jotted down the address before pulling off, as a reminder to try again. As I shifted into gear, something in the road caught my eye, and I glanced out my car window: The amiable cat sat at my car door, plaintive pretty eyes looking up at me. I put the car in park, opened the car door, and she jumped into my lap. Stroking her, I held her and peered into that stunning sweet face. I wanted so very much to help her and her offspring to avoid suffering. The kitten mortality rate in America is reported as high as 75% in one study. Most of her litter would likely not live to adulthood, and the surviving one or two weren't probably weren't going to spend their lives purring in someone's lap.

Reaching to the back seat, I pulled a crate forward to the passenger seat and put the cat in it. I turned the key again and drove away. I'd just found some stray cat wandering in the middle of a public road, right?

After spay and vaccinations and a day to recover, I returned the cat to her home. She popped out of the crate, looked around, sat down on the sidewalk in front of her home, and began grooming.

The lesson I learned? That in caring for animals, the correct decision isn't always outright clear to you. Considering our pet overpopulation in America, there are few valid reasons for anyone to resist having a pet cat or dog fixed. And no, it is not ethical to take a pet to surgery without the owner's permission. But is it ethical to have her in my arms and leave her behind in hopes that I will hear from an owner who I suspect doesn't even recall that she has a cat? This wasn't any sort of pedigreed cat, and she looked rough. Knowing that a spay would remarkably improve this cat's health and condition, plus prevent a litter that statistics said wouldn't thrive, I took her to surgery.

A few months later I drove by and the same feline was sleeping on the porch of the same dilapidated house with the same old gentleman passing the time in a chair. She was shiny, nicely fleshed out, and bright-eyed as she met my gaze, and at that moment I didn't regret what I had done.

People actually need to be reminded that pets cannot choose to stop breeding. I once asked a man what his cat's name was. "Her name 'Ho,'" he said, spitting with contempt. "She been with every tomcat here."

No cat or dog has ever been able to make a choice not to breed. Just give owners the facts: Animals are not humans. They cannot decide to reproduce or not. It is up to us to stop the cycle of suffering and overpopulation for them.

CHAPTER 21

Overnight Delivery

Double dilemma

LATE ONE SATURDAY afternoon we accepted a feral cat who had just been trapped in preparation for her spay surgery the next morning. Solid black, short shiny coat, gold eyes flashing in fear, the little cat cowered in the corner of the trap, hissing and spinning when her trap cover was raised. The barn owner reported she'd shown up at his barn a few months earlier. He agreed she could stay, and had accepted our offer of free spay surgery so there would be no kittens. He already had four barn cats. He'd not called us for this care, I had heard about this cat from his neighbor. With some convincing, the barn owner had agreed to trap her for surgery tomorrow.

We placed her, trap draped with a large towel, in a quiet corner of what would be the preoperative preparation and anesthesia room the next day. Then we finished setting up for the 100 cat spay/neuter surgeries we had scheduled.

Spay and neuter surgeries commenced at eight that morning, and we were moving along at a rapid pace; in total we'd had 111 cats show up, more than anticipated. It was hectic and busy. Then the tech administering anesthetic injections tapped me on the shoulder. The little black female feral cat had delivered one tiny kitten.

I huddled with one of the veterinarians. We wanted to save the kitten. But, how could we? The mother was a proven wild feral cat. She wasn't purring. She was ignoring the kitten. She was stressed, terrified, and just plain scared. It is not unusual for animals to reject their offspring under duress, and that loomed as a possibility.

If one of us took the wild cat and kitten home and detained them in a cage (this feral certainly couldn't reasonably be released in someone's home) for the six to eight weeks she'd need to raise the kitten, the cat would spend those weeks cowering in fear. Plus, I had no one willing or able to do that.

If we returned her fertile to the barn owner with her tiny kitten, our chances of trapping her and the kitten again in eight weeks were slim. And the mortality rate for a newborn kitten returning to a barn where temps would be in the 40-degree range at night would be extraordinarily high, to say nothing of death by foxes, coyotes, stray and feral dogs, other wildlife, and disease. Even if we did return the cat to her adopted barn and the kitten survived, we had so few volunteers to return in two months to try to catch them again. Plus, the property owner had done due diligence by trapping her, but I knew his patience wouldn't extend to taking back two cats, both of them still fertile, and doing it all again in two months.

Painful experience and years of statistics had already enlightened us: Both cat and kitten would likely be lost to follow-up if we returned them to that barn today. Even if we had a volunteer who would detain the mother cat and kitten in a cage for eight weeks and then bring them both to be fixed, I had no guarantee that the barn owner would take them back after that. Plus, they then would next have to be detained in a cage in his barn for a period long enough to convince them both that they had returned home. It would be like a new relocation after she'd been away that long. I knew the barn owner was not going to agree to set up and daily clean up a cage occupied with a wild cat and kitten for weeks while they adjusted. Socializing her kitten would be difficult too if it was, as needed, housed in the cage with its wild mother.

Another vet proposed her solution: She had friends who said they would adopt the kitten—in eight weeks, once it was able to leave its mother. They wouldn't take the kitten now though. Considering the innumerable times folks have smiled and told me they'll adopt an animal—after hearing its sad story—and then changed their minds the next day, I was willing to bet money that in two months when I called them to come get their kitten, they would not. That happy fuzzy warm virtuous feeling they had today would have long passed and they would say sorry, circumstances had changed, now they couldn't take him. At that time it would be June and area private and public shelters, even if I could find one that was taking cats and would accept one from our county, would already be euthanizing excess kittens. So I felt if this couple really wanted to help, they should take ownership today. We would support them in the effort and provide supplies, vet care, food. They declined.

Suppose we spayed the mother today and tried to raise the kitten alone? If separated from its mother, the kitten would require bottle feeding every two hours. For 24-hours a day. For probably two to three weeks. Only a person who doesn't have a job or many other obligations, and who doesn't need sleep can do that. I'm over eighty percent of the way to dead and I have never met that person. Even when someone can bottle feed, the kitten mortality rate is still exceptionally high. Kittens need to be nestled against their healthy mother to have any hope of growing up healthy themselves. They need colostrum, antibodies, immunity. They need their mother.

But the vet protested she'd already recruited a volunteer to bottle feed the kitten. My heart sank when I saw her nominee. Christine was a simple and sweet young woman with three children. Living with her second husband in a trailer, we'd met when she called for help getting her three female cats, one male cat, and 14 kittens fixed. Low-income and with only a sixth-grade education, Christine wasn't able to land a job. Even if she had, she didn't have a car and there is certainly no public transportation in rural MS. Living 12 miles from the nearest small town, Christine was dependent upon her sometimes abusive and volatile husband for a roof over her head and food on the table. I feared the consequences for her should Christine take home a tiny baby kitten who required exhausting bottle feeding.

But with no other good choices and in the midst of a bustling and hectic 100+ cat spay/neuter surgery clinic, we made the decision. We handed the tiny kitten, a bottle, and kitten milk replacer formula over to Christine. The mother cat was spayed. After an overnight stay, the mother cat was released to her barn. Sadly, the kitten did not survive.

These were painful lessons here for me, and maybe you've felt sadness or frustration or even anger reading this. We had no good choices. None. We had no one and no place to keep a wild, terrified, stressed feral cat while she raised a kitten. Even if we did, the mother and kitten might not have a home to return to. If they were able to return to the same barn, the mother cat might not recognize it (the kitten of course wouldn't) and both might flee when released, only to be struck by a car or killed by a dog. Both mother and kitten could be sickened from the stress of captivity. And so on. We chose what seemed to be the best option out of zero good ones.

You will be faced with painful no-win situations when you delve into animal welfare issues. You will not feel like a winner. You may even be reviled and flamed online. But you will have to fairly and objectively assess the issue, call experienced mentors for wisdom and input, and then make the decision that you believe is best for the animal. Maybe it won't be the right one. Maybe it will. Strive for the most optimal outcome you can expect with the information you have and the resources available at that time.

All hospitals and surgery centers have surgical supplies that are discarded clean and unused. Gauze pads, plastic bowls, hand towels, surgical gowns, skin staple guns, prep applicators, and unopened suture are just a few of the items tossed. Expired but unused and still sterile surgical gloves or other surgical items may be trashed too. Some efforts have been made to ship these supplies overseas to developing countries, but the cost is usually more than the value of the items, and the stuff may not be what the recipient needs anyway. If you know someone who works in surgery, ask if they can arrange to harvest for you these clean, unsoiled, and unused but discarded supplies, within the hospital's regulations of course. Some of these items you'll be able to utilize in a spay/neuter surgery clinic. Others you'll be able to offer to a veterinarian in barter or as a bonus thanks for care of an animal.

Orphan kitten Bertie being raised by surrogate mother CiCi; see Chapter 23.

CHAPTER 22

Bertie

Anonymous aid

"SOMEBODY PUT A kitten on my porch," Ms. Cutler stated in her voicemail that Sunday. "I thought yesterday maybe it was a mama cat that left it, but I haven't seen her if it is. This kitten real young, too tiny. Not old enough to eat. Anyway, something needs to be done or it's going to die soon."

A HARP volunteer had trapped and transported for spay/neuter surgery over 15 of the adult cats roaming Ms. Cutler's rural property. There had been nearly a dozen kittens too. Even though some of the kittens appeared healthy, placement had been difficult. Several only found adoptive homes after being transported to Northern states. Some sick kittens from Ms. Cutler's property, already blinded by a virulent feline herpes virus that attacked their eyes, had been euthanized.

Feline herpes virus is not transmissible to humans, but it is widespread and common in colonies of cats, especially unvaccinated cats. Cats who have the virus remain carriers for life. Adult cats may have enough natural immunity to stave off the disease, or at least be only mildly sickened, but kittens with their immature immune systems are precariously vulnerable. Malnourishment can allow a secondary bacterial eye infection to flourish and destroy the cornea and other delicate eye structures. When you see kittens with runny noses and discharge from eyes, you may suspect herpes virus, although remember it could just be a simple bacterial infection. You'll need a veterinarian to diagnose. We were confident though that these sickly kittens had herpes virus, and given the fact that most of them had already been blinded by it—confirmed by the veterinarian—we knew they could not live outdoors, nor were they likely to be adopted. Even if their vision could have been saved, and even if we'd had the funding and the time and the volunteers to care for them during for treatment, there remained the possibility that the kittens would experience a lifetime of thick, mucus-producing sneezing, accompanied by varying degrees of eye discharge. Not something owners enjoy in a housecat.

Ms. Cutler had been referred to us by a neighbor. While she wasn't indifferent to the cats, she lacked knowledge of even basic cat care principles. As an indigent minority woman living in rural MS, she had few options for helping them. She struggled to keep herself afloat. One could have made a persuasive argument that no cats should live there, as she had few funds and limited understanding of cat care. That however would mean you'd need to catch, euthanize, and bury the free roaming cats there. No one wanted to euthanize healthy cats and Ms. Cutler was willing to let them stay. She agreed to feed and water them daily, so we fixed the cats. HARP has provided cat food for her when she could not afford it, which is not ideal but is what it takes.

With the colony stabilized, we were dismayed to receive her call about an abandoned kitten that day. At least now though Ms. Cutler realized a tiny kitten alone needed help, and she had called for it. That was progress in her newly acquired knowledge that animals do suffer and action should be taken when they do.

The volunteer went to Ms. Cutler's house on a 95-degree hot, humid day, finding a tiny grey kitten, about 10 days old, lying unmoving in the yard. Ants swarmed over the 7-oz creature. We do not know if a mother cat did drop the kitten there, but we suspected not, as she was never seen. Ms. Cutler concluded someone most likely had placed the kitten on her property after discovering she had received help with her cats.

Knocking the ants off the tiny creature, the volunteer laid the kitten in a crate and drove her home. There she dripped water from a syringe into the kitten's mouth while I tried to reach our vet. Moribund, the dehydrated kitten seemed to be in need of euthanasia. However, before the vet returned my call the water rehydrated the kitten, who revived. A quick photo posted to Facebook yielded a fast offer from a cat rescue in another county to take and place the kitten. We rejoiced, and when the vet called, I told him we had successfully, miracle of miracles, placed the kitten and felt like the feline would be okay if we could sustain him with kitten milk replacer formula. The next day the vet examined the kitten and confirmed our plan.

Two days later the rescue rescinded their offer to take him. Like us, they had no fosterer available to bottle feed, which the kitten would require for another 2 weeks. Like us, they did not have a nursing mother cat who could feed the kitten. Like us, they did not have a home for him if he survived.

Crestfallen, we regrouped. After this tiny baby had rallied, was nursing a bottle and trying to walk, mewing for his mother or anyone who would hold him, it just seemed reprehensible to euthanize him. Of course, I ended up with him, as I had in my home three kittens who'd been abandoned at a commercial site on a busy highway. They were in my house awaiting growth and immunity so they could transition to my barn. In that room also was an aged barn cat who'd grown too infirm to leave outdoors, and a cat recovering from a fracture repair. Both mothered the kitten for me.

Bottle-feeding the little fellow for nearly two weeks, I was relieved when he finally started munching kitten chow with his new kitten friends. Named Bertie, the bundle of fluff grew fast, and owned our hearts as he grew.

Several lessons came out of Bertie's life. First, it just seems that an animal who has fought against odds to stay alive deserves a chance to make it work. Bertie was in the last hours of his life when the volunteer retrieved him. He latched onto a chance to live like he latched onto the nipple of the bottle offered him.

The second lesson was one I learned early on: Limit the number of people who know that you have a soft spot for animals. When I first started helping animals living with the poor, I'd come home to find a dog tied to my mailbox and confused cats huddled in my driveway. I paid the telephone company to remove my address from the phone book. I wouldn't give callers my last name and I never gave out my address; I started using a P. O. Box for mail. I've also learned to advise those we help with multiple animals to do the same, or at least not advertise that they've had free or low-cost help with animals.

This has to be balanced with our mission to spread the word about spay/neuter surgery. We do want them to let others know there is help available. But when caring for animals, be cautious lest the general public decide that you are operating an animal shelter or animal rescue in an area where none exists. In communities where a municipal animal shelter does exist, unexpected pets who turn up can be surrendered there if necessary. But in rural areas where there is no shelter, dumping an animal on someone else only transfers the problem to them, it doesn't solve the animal's welfare issue. We suspect neighbors or friends discovered Ms. Cutler had received help with her cats, and drew the conclusion that cats dumped there would get help.

Ask your local newspaper editor if he or she will donate space for a display ad detailing your nonprofit's message about spay/neuter services. You can find free prototypes of effective ads on internet animal welfare sites, then you just plug in your info. If you can't get a display ad run as a public service, consider sending the newspaper a Press Release about your organization's activities. Follow the format you'll find on the internet to make your Press Release look professional. Attach a crisp sharp photograph featuring one of the animals you've helped. It's free advertising if they run it, and a well written professional looking document boosts the chance of getting the message out. An eye-catching animal photograph alongside will draw reader attention to your article.

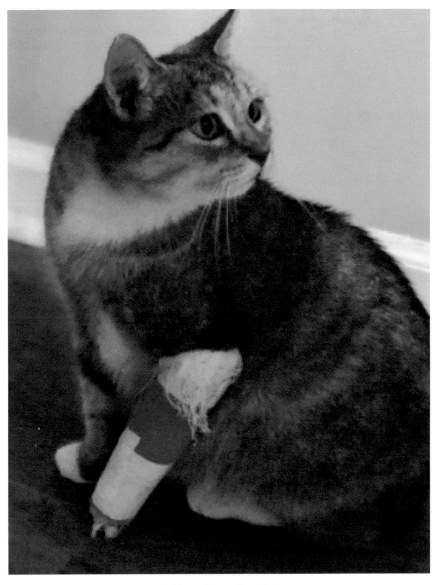

CiCi's newly straightened leg

CHAPTER 23

CiCi

A broke leg

"KNOW ANYONE WHO wants a cat? It's a real nice cat," asked the workman as he gathered his tools from his truck at my barn entrance.

"Sorry, no. Everybody who wants a cat has one," I replied.

"Yes, but this is a real sweet cat. She showed up at my neighbor's house. My neighbor is elderly, and she's been feeding this cat. She wouldn't turn her away, but she just can't keep her," he continued.

"Get in line," I sighed. "This time of year—summertime—shelters and rescues are overflowing with cats and kittens. A lot of those will be beautiful, friendly, high pet-quality cats. Competition for homes is fierce. There just hasn't ever been an American who wanted a cat but couldn't find one."

Undeterred, he explained that the cat had arrived with three kittens in tow, kittens he estimated were about three months old. Later, two of the kittens who were social and friendly vanished. No telling what happened there. Maybe a kind person helped two friendly kittens to find loving permanent homes after they were fixed. Maybe someone not so kind snatched them. Only the mother cat and her third kitten remained, he continued. Describing the third kitten as feral, saying it couldn't be touched, he repeated they needed a home. I reiterated that I knew of no homes available. I certainly had no vacancy myself.

"What if I helped this lady get the cat and kitten fixed and vaccinated? Think she could keep her then?" I proposed.

"Nah, she wouldn't keep her. She doesn't want a cat," he replied.

Then he mentioned the cat's leg.

"She's got a broke leg but she gets around fine," he added.

"The cat has a broken leg?"

"Yeah, but it's no problem. She can get around fine," he explained, as if discussing a bump on the shin.

That did it for me. The thought of a homeless hungry mother cat wandering the streets with her three kittens, dragging a broken leg while looking for food and shelter, tore up my heart. I've had a broken bone. It hurts. And a handicapped cat living outdoors and roaming for food? Being bred over and over even with a fractured leg? There was a good chance this cat could become dinner herself before her next litter.

I made a decision. Worst case scenario: I could have the cat euthanized to end the misery of homelessness and a broken leg. Best case: The leg could be repaired and she'd live in my barn. I sighed and told him I'd take her. But I explained I needed him to get her to me ASAP.

"If her kittens are three months old, she is already pregnant again. You have to get her to me quickly so she can see a doctor. I'll take her and her kitten, but I'm not taking eight cats when she has another litter," I insisted. Loaning him a humane trap to catch the remaining kitten, I instructed him in safe, minimal stress trapping procedures.

"Sure. I can bring them Friday," he said, stowing the trap in his truck.

Friday came and went. I called and left him a message that I was awaiting the cats but timing was critical. The next week I called and left him another voicemail. And the next. He never returned my calls. I gave up, assuming something had happened to both the cats or maybe he'd found a home closer to him.

Two months later he returned to perform more work at my barn. I asked about the cats.

"Oh, that kitten is gone. Don't know what happened to it," he said.

The mother cat?

"She's still there. I just didn't know if you still would take her so I didn't bring her today. She's pregnant now."

"Get her to me, and I'll get her to a vet. Let him decide what is best for her," I replied, angry as his casual apathy regarding a pregnant, injured animal. "But we need to do that immediately. I am still willing to take her, but no one needs any more kittens. That's just way too much of a good thing."

Two days later he called to say he didn't have the time to transport her to me. So I drove across two counties to his neighbor's home to pick up the cat.

What I saw in the crate handed to me was a depressed, thin, short-hair grey, white, and orange cat, with a protuberant sagging belly and a dull coat. No purring, little interest in me. She leaned lopsidedly on the healed but deformed break in her left front leg. With the fracture untreated, her leg bent at a right angle, where the ends of the fractured bones had fused.

Spayed a few days later, we were able to prevent another litter, and she recovered promptly. With a healthy new diet and a safe place to rest, her personality began to shine through. She did ambulate without much difficulty, but she was using the fracture site to bear her weight, which caused an uneven shoulder-up-shoulder-down seesaw gait. The fractured leg bones seemed to have melded together like they were fixed in concrete. Her doctor wanted her to recover from the spay surgery before we tackled the leg. He explained a kick had most likely broken the leg, whether from a large animal or a person. Could have been an auto crash but with no other injuries, that seemed less likely. Amputation loomed as a logical choice, since the fracture was at least several months old and the bones were already fused at an unnatural angle. However, he wanted to try first to save the leg. We could always amputate later if the repair failed.

The choice of surgical fixation versus amputation at least in part depends upon the animal's disposition and temperament. Cats are more generally more likely than dogs to rest and allow a fracture to heal, but any fractious cat or dog can destroy a delicate, tedious, fracture pinning in an instant. Named CiCi for crippled cat, she had the disposition of a compliant and pleasant patient. Easy to handle, she was one of those cats who would allow a child to carry her around. That made her a good candidate for a repair. And she was a good patient, sailing easily through the surgery. She never picked at or bothered her splint, which was changed weekly for several months. Pain medication kept her comfortable after the surgery.

The surgeon had to first excise the fused bone from the untreated fracture, then insert a pin to hold the fresh cut surfaces together. CiCi was quiet and cooperative with every treatment and became a favorite with the clinic staff. You get a cat like that, you're on her side, you're want to be on her team. You root for her. This care only could be provided though because her doctor signed on to her team too, and performed this delicate time-consuming surgery at a modest fee that I could afford. God bless him.

The lesson here is often told: That which is not easily treated had better be prevented. Litters of kittens are hard to place; it is far easier to spay a cat even during gestation than try to place any surviving kittens eight weeks later. And a long-neglected fracture is trickier and more complicated to treat than a fresh one. In fact, it may not be repairable.

Apparently, no one offered this cat a ride to a doctor when she was first injured. Even after I offered to help, it was two months before I met the cat. My bitterness surfaces. But not everyone has been blessed as you and I have—with a car, gas money, and with a heart drawn to these enchanting creatures. The elderly woman at whose home this cat settled said she couldn't afford a vet bill and didn't want a cat anyway. There is no humane society or animal welfare group in that community who might have been contacted to help. But even if someone had driven the injured cat to a vet, and the vet had offered care for the unwanted homeless animal, the vet likely couldn't place or keep the cat either. Even if the vet had offered euthanasia, this woman was reportedly unable or unwilling to spend money on a cat. In most rural counties here, the woman would also have been required to take the remains with her for burial.

Once I visited the regal, stately, luxury home of a well-to-do businessman. On his golf cart rested a splendid, long-haired black cat. As I stroked the graceful creature, the homeowner mentioned she had not been feeling well, wasn't getting around well, and he hypothesized that the cat was ill.

"Surely there is a vet around here who could look at her," I said, alarmed.

"A vet? I didn't pay any money for that cat," he exclaimed, frowning at me as if I'd sprouted a third eye smack dab in the middle of my forehead. "I'm sure not spending any money on it."

This is why we hope you will help animals and why spay/neuter surgery is so important as your mission: It stops the flow of unwanted and homeless animals. Reducing the overpopulation of pets who suffer like this and are seen as having no value is a benefit of spay/neuter.

Keep a database of the people whose animals you help. Enter notes about no-shows, how many animals were fixed, any concerns you had. Once we qualified a cat for a free neuter after the owner produced documentation of public assistance and pleaded for help getting him fixed. One month after we neutered and vaccinated the cat at no charge, she presented the cat at an area veterinary clinic and paid to have him declawed. The vet was one of our volunteers, who had donated his time and skills to neuter the cat at no charge to her. When the owner arrived at his clinic with the paperwork we'd provided at neuter to prove the cat had been vaccinated, that understandably aggravated him. He felt our screening for eligibility had been inadequate if she qualified for a free neuter but could pay for declawing. We were equally dismayed that she claimed poverty on an essential cat health procedure—neuter—but suddenly had money for a procedure many consider cruel, and which has been banned in some areas. We had to decline to fix any more cats for her.

CHAPTER 24

Annie Lee

Deceiving appearances

"THAT DOG'S GOTTA go," proclaimed my spouse. He was staring at the yellow-eyed snarling dog who'd just walked up our driveway from the road. The dog stared back.

Looking like a Chocolate Lab, about 60 or 70 pounds, she had a close-cropped, shiny brown coat, spindly legs, and a boney spine with nearly each vertebra visible. The bulging distended tell-tale belly of pregnancy completed her appearance. The dog stepped forward two more steps, flashing golden eyes that seemed creepily yellow. Then she stopped and pulled her lips back in that fierce and threatening snarl again, exposing sharp, sparkly white teeth. Or at least it looked like a savage snarl. It certainly appeared ferocious enough to propel us both back a few steps, and ferocious enough to make us wish she wasn't this close to us.

But as we slowly and ever so carefully retreated, the dog's tail began to wag while she kept her lips retracted in that bare the teeth snarl-like position. We finally realized she was grinning at us, as our dear dog friends do. We melted, and she began to twist herself in half, wriggling with joy using her whole body, all while maintaining the snarling appearance.

Apparently, this dog had an unsettling habit of pulling her lips up so taut that it seemed she was issuing a menacing warning to you. Those yellowish eyes completed the scary look.

This was Labor Day weekend. Dumping of cats and dogs is more common on long holiday weekends, maybe because people have more free time to load up their unwanted animals and give them a ride out of town. We had no animal shelter in our area then, and wouldn't for years. For rural homeowners in this community, the choices would be:

Drive the dog further down the road and push her out so she'd be someone else's problem. Nope, not even on our options list.

Shoot her and be done with it. Of course, we wouldn't consider that.

Shoo her off, try to drive her away and back down to the road, encouraging her to try her luck at someone else's house. No to that too. She was obviously pregnant and if we didn't help her, this litter might be born in the woods. If the pups survived, they would likely turn feral, becoming unsocialized, wild, intact, roaming dogs.

Bed her down for the weekend, next business day take her to my vet and pay for euthanasia, then bring her back and bury her. We didn't do this either, because she looked young and healthy, other than being thin. Euthanasia wasn't warranted, especially if she could get along with our other animals.

Try to place her on Petfinder.com, which was one of only a few pet adoption networking options for reaching beyond our own community 16 years ago. As she appeared to be a purebred Chocolate Lab, we felt like that could work. That's the choice we made.

Once we determined she could get along with our cats, horses, and other dogs, I photographed her and posted her to Petfinder. This was a frustrating task, because we had only a slow and unreliable dial-up landline at that time and it would often lose the connection before a photo was transmitted. I also took her to be spayed after the holiday so she'd be ready for the person who wanted to adopt her.

While waiting and hoping for a responsible adopter we discovered this dog's look was a fabulous built-in personal safety and security feature. She greeted any visitors to our property with yellow-looking eyes flashing, lips pulled up taut, that mouthful of big shiny razor-like teeth exposed. Folks hopped back into their cars real fast, slamming and locking the door. Worked great on traveling salesmen and all those other pesky peddlers who come to your door. Everyone beat a hasty retreat. That's all we had to do, was send Annie Lee out to greet them. Then stand at the window and smile and wave as they left us in peace while the dog wondered why they wouldn't get out and pet her.

We fell so in love with her that I removed her Petfinder posting and we claimed her as ours. She never chased our horses, she ignored the cats, and she enjoyed our other dogs. We named her Annie Lee, after Mrs. Annie Lee Roberts, an extraordinary woman who loved both Texas history and animals. Born Annie Lee Warren in Texas in 1895, she later married businessman Summer-field Roberts, and the couple moved to Dallas, where they prospered financially. Wanting to help animals throughout the world, including wildlife and domesticated animals, Ms. Roberts witnessed events as a child that shaped her beliefs on animal welfare as an adult. Growing up she observed firsthand the mistreatment of circus animals and farm animals, and it changed her life. Once as a little girl she intervened when she saw a farmer mercilessly beating his plow horse. Described as one the 'gentlest and kindest people you've ever known,' she later became a philanthropist, and The Summerlee Foundation was founded in 1988. In addition to supporting Texas History, the Foundation works to alleviate fear, pain and suffering of animals and to promote animal protection and the prevention of cruelty to animals. In fact, at that time, as I began helping animals living with the poor, our fledging organization had received support from The Summerlee Foundation, and so we decided to honor Mrs. Roberts' memory by naming this gentle sweet dog Annie Lee. After all, she seemed to embody Ms. Roberts' personality—gentle and kind, but with an underlying fierceness.

Our cherished dog Annie Lee lived with us for another 12 years, and still I shake my head in disbelief at the numbskull who dumped such a loving, gorgeous companion in the countryside. How could this person have tossed such treasure out like trash? I assume he or she didn't want the litter, or maybe couldn't afford a large dog spay. But Annie Lee sure appeared to be a purebred Chocolate Lab, and one would suspect someone paid money for her. If you can afford to buy a dog, you should be able to afford the care.

Maybe he found for some reason (divorce is a common theme here) he couldn't keep her, and word wafted to him that I was involved in animal welfare, so he dumped her at my driveway. I'll never know. We adored this dear placid creature, as did the all of the other animals here. She loved to run with the other dogs alongside my horse as I rode, but as she aged, she just became too old and arthritic to go the distance. Wanting so badly to travel the trail with us, she would gamely limp along, but would eventually fall behind the pack, and she finally became too infirm to go. So, before I set out on horseback, I'd bed her down in the house, then sneak out to ride. When I returned from the trail, I'd stop the horse at the back door, then run in and let Annie Lee out. Climbing back up on the horse, I'd ride the last short distance to the barn. Annie Lee would lumber along with us, grinning and wagging. Then I'd congratulate her as always for having gone "the whole way" with us. She'd pull up her lips in that bright smile, which will forever make me grin too when I remember her.

The lesson this sweet dog Annie Lee taught me is how deceiving appearances can be. Even we initially fell victim to that toothy "snarl" greeting, although we came to love it. So many others though couldn't see past her face, failing to peer beyond the fierce facade to realize her tail was wagging and she was dancing in delight at the sight of you.

Another lesson we hope will come from Annie Lee's life is that through the actions of the volunteers of the Homeless Animals Relief Project more people will realize they don't have to abandon animals. They may be able to get help with caring for pets—low cost or free spay/neuter surgery, perhaps assistance with food, or help with providing basic medical care for their pets. That's why we need more volunteers like you.

But most of all, we hope that more people will lead lives that follow Mrs. Roberts' example, and become advocates, interventionists, and philanthropists (big or small) for suffering animals who cannot speak for themselves.

We received a call from a low-income woman whose female dog we had spayed a few years earlier. She had three male dogs now she said. Intact (not neutered), the dogs had a vicious fight over a neighbor's female dog in heat four days earlier. The most grievously injured dog was now unable to stand, and his substantial wounds leaked pus and blood, she said. Pleading for our help with veterinary care, she said she had no money to pay.

I instantly agreed we would cover the cost of having a vet examine the suffering dog, we would pay for humane euthanasia if deemed necessary, and we could cover basic care if he could be saved. Our stipulation was, as always, that if we cover the cost of professional veterinary care for an injured or sick pet, the animal is to be spayed or neutered before release to the owner if it survives. Had this woman's male dogs been neutered, they likely wouldn't have fiercely fought over a female dog in heat. But the owner refused to allow a neuter if the dog survived. She refused the offer. I am still as stunned today as I was then: To her, the dog's testicles were more important than his beating heart, his suffering, and his life.

*Cat found wandering on a major highway at age 3
weeks; mother and littermates never found.*

CHAPTER 25

Iris

Next house down

AS WE PULLED off a busy highway into the derelict trailer park, we counted about a dozen cats roaming the bleak, littered landscape. We'd come to canvass the enclave and offer free spay/neuter surgery to the pets of residents living there. But the first person we saw was a balding, pot-bellied guy with deep brown leathery and wrinkled skin. Dressed in frayed sagging shorts and a tattered t-shirt, he turned out to be the manager. Not looking in much better condition than some of the animals scampering around, he stepped from behind a vacant trailer. Swinging from his right hand, held by the scruff of her neck, was a pregnant pastel (pale, diluted colors like grey, cream, and white) calico cat. Her gravid belly lolled in front of her, but she remained quiet, placid, and limp in his grip. Her eyes met ours then rolled up to try to meet her captor's.

"What's going on with that cat?" we asked, approaching him.

"What are you all doin'?" he retorted suspiciously, stopping. The cat still hung limp in his grip.

"We're offering free birth control surgery to the cats and dogs here," I rushed to explain, thrusting a card with information on our nonprofit at him. He didn't take the card, so I pocketed it and reached for the cat. He snatched her back before I felt fur. She continued to watch us and seemed totally unperturbed by her predicament.

"Don't want these cats here fixed," he snorted. "Need lots of 'em to control the mice and snakes."

The volunteer with me, way cooler than me, interjected with a simple, rational explanation about animal overpopulation and animal suffering, but he cut her off too.

"We don't want you here. You need to leave. Now I got things to do," and he marched off, the cat still hanging in his grip.

We visit trailer parks in rural MS because they are a source of fertile pets. Low-income residents of dilapidated trailer parks cannot afford $300 to fix and provide basic care for a pet, and so pets overpopulate in low-income areas. Another reason pets overpopulate distressed communities is that the destitute, who live in such desolate circumstances, are more generous than the rich. Check that claim against IRS records of giving: As income rises, charitable giving plummets. Fact: The more people make, the less they give. A revealing statistic some years back showed a state in the Northeast ranked number two in the list of America's richest states. But it tumbled to 49th in charitable giving. In that same list, Mississippi was the 49th poorest state, but soared to second in giving in America. Turns out low-income people give at nearly twice the rate of their wealthier counterparts.

Our experience is that less fortunate people seem more likely to try to provide for an animal who's also not faring so well. Maybe it's empathy. Sharing leftovers with a starving animal seems to come naturally to legions of poor, and they are more accustomed to the sight of wandering, homeless animals. While the poor may lack the resources to care for a homeless animal, many are just like you and I, they bond with these animals and do what they can for them.

So it is disheartening to hear well-to-do pet owners proclaim that it is the fault of an animal if it is homeless.

"There's a reason you see those mongrel dogs on the side of the road," sniffed a woman with two expensive purchased purebred dogs. Pontificating that all pitiful side-of-the-road dogs are ill behaved, rowdy, unmanageable, or diseased, she concluded, "That's why nobody wants them. That's why they get put out."

You and I counter that it isn't the dog or cat's behavior that led him or her to that sad fate, it is the *owner's* behavior. Or the community's behavior in ignoring the plight of the homeless animals. And then there are the municipal leaders who slash the budget that promotes community health, and eliminate best practices animal welfare management. Abandoned and starving cats and dogs are victims of cruelty at worst and negligence at best. But the animals are absolutely, positively, not the ones behaving badly in this situation.

It's also not uncommon for farmers to reject our offers of free care for barn cats. Misconceptions include the belief that cats won't go after mice in the barn if they are fed, so owners withhold food. Others believe that cats shouldn't be sterilized, because their barn will need plenty of cats to keep the reptiles and rodents under control. This reveals a skewed and inaccurate perception of cat care; they are unaware of how exponentially cats reproduce, and they don't realize cats who are busy breeding and reproducing have little time for hunting. Either they don't know or don't care how much suffering is involved in breeding, pregnancies, littering, malnutrition, and disease. You can offer education and enlightenment.

So, I trotted after this man as he continued towards the highway.

"Let me just hold the cat while we talk," I said, trying again to wrest the cat from him. He ignored me and walked on.

"What are you going to do with her?" I quizzed, hurrying to keep up.

"Gonna toss her in that ditch," he said, pointing with his free hand to a ravine across the busy highway. "She ain't no good. Won't hunt. Spends her days hangin' around with people here in their trailers. Don't need a lazy cat."

"Give her to me, why don't you?" I replied, growing desperate as we closed in on the highway where traffic sped past. "I want a cat. Please can I have this one?"

"Yours," he said, abruptly whirling and shoving the cat at me. The cat's neck fur snapped back into place as he released her, and I felt her placidly settle into my arms. "Now you all go on."

"But we'd like to get these cats here fixed," my colleague reiterated.

"I said no," he retorted, and walked off. "Go on, get out, both of you. I mean it."

We put the remarkably relaxed and "too friendly" cat into a crate in the car. Not indignant in the least, she smoothed her fur and curled up comfortably as we drove off the property.

Turning into the first private driveway that bordered the trailer park, we found a homeowner who wasn't nearly as interested in having lots of cats overflowing onto his property. He readily offered access to set our traps there.

That weekend we placed traps along the fence line between the trailer park and this house. We caught 12 cats as they wandered from the trailer park. Following the scent of the fast food fried chicken we'd purchased for the traps, they stepped right in. After spay/neuter surgery, ear tipping, vaccination, and recovery, the cats were released again to go about their lives in the trailer park. That trailer park owner seemed none the wiser and probably never noticed the cat's ears had been tipped.

One could argue that euthanasia for the cats, most of whom had no known owner, would have been kinder. After all, the manager had proven himself to be unkind. But the cats we trapped were shiny, in excellent body condition, and were obviously being fed by the residents. Living in a run-down trailer park is never, ever, going to be the life you or I would choose for cats. It is however the life they've been given, and we made the decision to trap-neuter-return.

But we had no potential adopters for this dear sweet pregnant cat, and had to call upon a man we knew who loved cats, and ask him to add her to his family. After spay surgery she was named Iris and lived with him for years. We got a sweet note from him several months after her placement: "Iris has given me more love than two ex-wives ever did." After her death, he buried her in a grave marked with a rectangle of white rocks.

The lesson Iris taught me is patience. She resisted not as this guy held her in his grip, awaiting a better plan. And as she was patient, so were we. When the trailer park owner refused our offer of help, we didn't fight a futile argument with him. We went to his neighbor, who was more than happy to help us meet our goals of fixing the cats in the trailer park next door. Patience gives one the time to come up with alternatives and work-arounds when someone blocks your path.

Spay/neuter surgery, fixing pets early, before they have even one litter, is the sustainable, cost-effective answer to this dilemma of homeless cats. Preventing homelessness and the need for rescue of lost, hurting, or sick pets starts with animal birth control surgery.

If there is no low-cost spay/neuter surgery program in your area, then search for an existing veterinary clinic who'll perform the surgeries, or will let you work there when the clinic is closed to the public. In rural areas with neither a program or an available clinic, you may have to set up your own spay/neuter facility. Unfortunately, we have counties in Mississippi that have no veterinary clinic. Dream big but start small and think manageable. Improvise when possible to allow more money for the animals' care. We received a grant to purchase a used 34-foot travel trailer with three slide-outs for $15,000, then we removed most of the furniture. We didn't purchase a $2500 surgery table, we bought $39 plastic tables at the dollar store and elevated them on $10 bed risers to the proper height. We didn't buy $600 surgical instrument packs; we bought the $99 clearance specials. We skipped the $900 surgical light and acquired two $150 medical lamps that work just as well. An inhalation anesthesia machine was purchased used but certified on eBay. We have oxygen (donated), emergency resuscitation equipment, intravenous therapy supplies. Our autoclave sits on the kitchen counter, next to the sink where soiled instruments are cleaned and prepared for sterilization. The covered stove serves as a mini office desk; the dinette is our "lounge." While our setup isn't fancy, you'll find we're better equipped for safe surgeries than a lot of professional facilities, and our mortality/morbidity rate reflects that. Clean, unused, but discarded and donated hospital surgical supplies save us money. A state licensed veterinarian performs the surgeries, we sometimes invite advanced veterinary medicine students to assist. When we work in this spay/neuter surgery trailer it costs us about $10 to neuter a cat. We only need a few syringes, some small doses of anesthetics, clippers, scrub solution, surgical gloves, two tiny surgical clips, and volunteers. Add suture, a pack of surgical instruments, skin glue, tattoo ink, and a few more drugs, but still the cost to spay a female cat isn't a lot higher. The trailer is parked in a donated spot on private property, so we meet owners with their pets at a public place and transport from there.

Travel trailer spay/neuter clinic setup. Surgery at table on left, recovery on table at right.

CHAPTER 26

Rhoda

All of creation

SLAMMING ON THE brakes, I braced and grimaced as the seat belt squeezed hard and restrained me from flying forward. Thankfully, there was no horrific thump or bump. I shifted into park and got out to look. A slender, diminutive, black and white tuxedo cat (so called because they are black with white chest and paws) scampered away, then leaped up the clay embankment that constituted the right side of the country road. I heaved a sigh of relief and stilled my trembling hands; I had not struck her. She eyeballed me with an indignant 'you almost killed me' glare.

She'd dashed in front of me as I approached the curve on the quiet isolated road. With the nearest homes at least a half-mile away, I could assume she was wandering, lost, or had been dumped. I turned back to the car, but stopped as the cat locked her green eyes on mine.

"You scared me, cat," I admonished. "Stay out of the road. It's dangerous!"

She stretched, circled, switched her tail, then descended from her perch on the embankment. Her gaze remained fixed on me.

"Hungry?" I asked. No response, just the cool scrutiny of this little feline. Pulling a container of dry cat food from the back of my car, I approached her. She retreated a few steps, then circled back to me.

Should I put down a pile of dry cat food and say a prayer for her wellbeing, and then go on my way? Could I leave a hungry socialized cat out in the middle of nowhere? Given her relaxed body language, her upright furling tail, her eyes meeting mine, and her approach to me, I knew she wasn't wild. Her demeanor suggested comfort with humans.

You and I are inclined to help the creature. But because everyone who wants a cat has one, I understood I probably couldn't place her if I took her home. Experiences thirty years past have taught me that the person who puts a stray dog or cat in their car is the odds-on favorite to pay the animal's bills, make difficult decisions about the animal's future, or end up as the animal's owner or guardian for the rest of his or her life. If I put her in my car, I should assume I'd just adopted another cat.

My decision-making process that afternoon was prejudiced. This cat was hanging out around one mile from my house. Of course, she would be fertile. Spayed or neutered cats don't get dumped or abandoned nearly as often as fertile animals, because they don't engage in the behaviors that annoy, such as littering and spraying and fighting. I didn't want a fertile cat roaming in my neighborhood; I couldn't bear to think of the litters born and dying in the woods. I didn't want to see the vultures picking over their remains in the road when they'd been hit. I didn't want to see starving cats, searching for any crumb of food, clawing through a fast food take-out bag tossed on the roadside.

I pulled a pet crate from the car, shook the bag of cat food, and the dainty creature sprinted for me, confirming that she knew a feeding routine. She zipped straight into the crate when I put some food in it. I closed the door as she gulped the food down whole.

At my home, I settled her into a spare bedroom. Instantly friendly, she acted like my new BFF. Not long on the wandering road, she had a shiny coat and glistening emerald eyes. I photographed her and posted her for adoption that night on our group's Petfinder page, but never got a nibble. I did get a surprise from her the next day, though.

Upon entering the room, I found the cat—named Rhoda now—on her side, in distress. Breathing fast, she was straining and pushing blood and embryonic tissue from her vagina. She was having a miscarriage. I called the vet—it was a Sunday afternoon and the offices were closed—but was advised to monitor her and call back if she didn't complete the miscarriage on her own. I was also to bring her to the clinic in the morning for evaluation.

Rhoda did miscarry her litter within an hour, then popped back to her feet to resume eating. Although she acted like nothing had happened, her bleeding continued, and she required urgent spay surgery the next morning. Rhoda survived and lives with me to this day. While she had no kittens herself, she's been an excellent foster-type mother to the kittens who pass through my care.

Two lessons Rhoda taught me: One, help animals on the spot when you can do so safely. Had Rhoda lived somewhere other than close to me, admittedly I might have put down some food and departed. If she'd appeared feral, I likely would have left some food but moved on when I realized I couldn't easily grab her. I am so glad I picked her up though, because had Rhoda experienced her miscarriage in those woods, the smell of blood and the sounds of her laboring would have drawn predators like coyotes who would have killed her. Even if she had found a safe haven for the event, the continuing flow and scent of her blood would have cost her the capacity to survive. She required an urgent spay to stop her bleeding. Without it she would not have lived. Maybe it was not a coincidence that a near crash alerted me to her presence that day.

The other thing I learned from Rhoda is how closely all of creation is related. As I cleaned up the expelled remains of her miscarriage, I pondered with wonder and sadness the embryonic kittens. The disproportionately large head, the gelatinous almost transparent shape, the barely formed extremities that resembled hands and feet, that large round dark eye. It looked so much like the photos we've all seen of a human embryo. I know feline embryos and human embryos are different; let me be crystal clear I'm not claiming equality here. But my goodness, we sure look a lot alike shortly after conception. That amazing sight still astounds me.

Rhoda taught me that the great divide between animal life and human life actually isn't that great. Let us inform others.

A female kitten born in April will come into her heat cycle the first time that summer, while she's still playing with her littermates. She'll be preparing to deliver her first litter that fall, while her owners are still calling her a kitten. She'll have her next litter the following spring. At one year of age, if she hasn't had obstetric complications or contracted deadly disease or injuries during breeding, she'll deliver her third litter that summer, and her fourth litter in the fall. Do the math: One female cat had six kittens one fall. Say three live, and each of them has four kittens the next spring, and now there are 16 cats. The kittens of the four spring kittens each have four kittens that fall, along with the original cat's spring, summer, and fall litters, and her first and second-generation offspring's litters, and now there are over 50 cats. There actually won't be that many though, because numerous kittens will succumb to malnutrition, injuries, and disease. Early age spay/ neuter stops all of this. While a good strong female cat can deliver 10-15 kittens per year, a male cat can father dozens more. Both males and females need to be fixed before five months of age to stop the cycle. Had the cat in the example been fixed before five months of age, all of this suffering and overpopulation would have stopped that very day. Be the one to do it.

CHAPTER 27

Truck Stop

Team or solo

WE GOT AN email from a long-distance trucker who'd discovered a dozen or so feral cats living behind a major truck line terminal. He'd called rescues and shelters around the area for help with getting them fixed, but no one returned his calls. Because this truck terminal was over 40-miles from us, I suggested several other organizations he could try. No luck. Most humane organizations don't want to deal with feral cats. These wild, free-roaming cats are not pets and can't be made into them. Feral kittens caught before the age of 6-8 weeks can often be tamed and become household pets. But right now, these cats needed to be fixed. A feeding station set up at the back of the truck terminal indicated the cats were being fed and watered, and they seemed to be in reasonably good condition according to the photos he sent. He'd not seen any kittens.

I called the truck line's office, where the circuitous recording repetitively demanded I choose team or solo before going further. After punching "0" three times, I finally got a live person on the line: "Team or solo?" she inquired. Explaining that I wasn't a trucker, neither team nor solo, I told her my call regarded the feral cats living on the property. She punted me to the voice message system for the terminal manager. No surprise, he never returned my calls.

Then we moved on to the next step, the 'scout it out' option. Another volunteer and I drove to the site. Next to the truck terminal was a farm products supply dealer, and next to that, a lane of low-income homes. Those backed up to an impoverished neighborhood filled with deserted houses, decaying trailers, and pronounced poverty.

We spoke with the farm supply dealer and found him amenable to getting the cats fixed. He had no qualms about allowing them to stay. Cats kept the rodent population from destroying feedstuffs, and reduced the number of snakes who zipped out of the fields behind the business, he explained. Getting the cats fixed would be a bonus.

Next we visited the seven houses lining the lane, five of which had bowls of water and cat food on their porches. At these houses the owners welcomed us and signed on to get the cats fixed too. At an abandoned house further down, thin cats slinked out through broken windows. One peered out from the dirt underneath the crumbling building.

We pulled back onto the road and drove around to the entrance to the neighborhood that abutted the commercial area. A teeming mass of humanity thronged through the streets on that cool spring Saturday afternoon, everyone enjoying one of the first sunny days after a hard winter. Wary eyes though followed the appearance of two white ladies pulling into the predominantly minority neighborhood. People went inside and closed their doors.

We saw cats racing for cover as we eased down the street; we approached residents and began handing out our cards. One guy flagged us down, explaining his mother had about 30 cats living around her house on the next block. He raced to tell her the good news: We would fix the cats for free. Five minutes later he was back. No, she wouldn't see us and no she wouldn't accept help. She knew the cats needed to be fixed and claimed she would do that herself. Of course, she couldn't. Nobody living in a decaying splintered house in a ghetto can afford to get 30 cats vetted. Even if she worked out a deal for a discount with a vet, she'd still be out hundreds, or most likely, thousands. We knew she couldn't afford it and wouldn't accomplish it. First, she'd need crates, then she'd need a car. She had neither. We were not able to help her cats. There was just too much suspicion and distrust of us. Her son was disappointed, as were we.

Skittles with her kittens

One resident had a lovely, gregarious white/grey tabby cat named Skittles. We'd knocked on the homeowner's door when we saw the kittens in her garage, but no answer. Spotting the cheerful adult cat across the road, we picked her to speak to her, and that got the owner out the door and into our faces. Although reluctant, she allowed us to take Skittles and her kittens with us for spay/neuter surgery. Two days later when the fixed and vaccinated cats were returned, again there was no answer at the door, so I left the animals at their home. An hour after that the owner left a soft, shy, sweet voice mail message for us, brimming with gratitude, thanking us for helping her cats.

Our tour of the neighborhood left no doubt that the animal overpopulation issue far exceeded our ability to help. The excess dogs and cats constituted an animal control issue beyond anything we could possibly offer. So many unowned animals, so many homeless. Most unsocialized, fearful. To catch all of them and transport for surgery would be a monumental undertaking. And performing spay/neuter surgery, then returning homeless creatures to roam and hunt for food and water and shelter is not only not ideal, it could be considered unethical. Gathering up these animals, getting them fixed, and then trying to place them far exceeded our abilities, and there were few homes available anyway. Most of these dogs and cats were poorly socialized or wild—not pets. And even if we did try to round up, shelter, and adopt out these animals, the time spent on that rescue and rehab would take us from our spay/neuter mission. More animals would be born even as we were trying to help the existing animals. We were forced to focus instead on the cats who'd just signed up for spay/neuter surgery.

But another volunteer thought there might be a way to help. He made more calls, hoping to locate a closer animal welfare advocate or organization that would help with trapping and transportation of owned animals or the feral cats at the truck terminal. A few hours later he called me, announcing he'd discovered a solution.

"This guy will trap them, drive them to the vet, and return them to the truck terminal or wherever we want them to go," he said.

"So what organization is he with?" I asked. This could be a solution, but always dig deeper when someone claims to have an easy way out. "How much does he charge?"

"I didn't get the name of his group. But he's the one to help us. I'm sure he won't charge anything, because he only wants to help animals. He'll do all the work. Sounded like a really nice guy," he replied.

If anything sounds too good to be true, it probably is. I called the man. Turns out he's a professional trapper. Yes, he traps cats, among other creatures. There would be a $27 per cat fee, and yes, he would drive them to the vet of our choice; that added a hefty mileage fee. If we just wanted them relocated, he would trap them and release them wherever we wanted, or put them on his 100-acre property. For another fee.

"Now by law I can't spay the females, but I can castrate the males," he continued. "The females, I just let them go. Plenty of room out here."

He said he was retired, and loved animals, so he earned his living now picking up unwanted cats and dogs or wildlife and releasing them on his acreage. Fertile was fine with him.

Appalled that he would release fertile cats, I asked if he'd considered how explosive cat population growth would impact the ecology and wildlife of his property. He waved that monumental concern away. I did not ask him how he castrated male cats. I already knew. Because he wasn't a veterinarian, he would have no access to DEA controlled anesthetic or sedating agents. That could only mean that he restrained the friendly male cats in a cruel fashion and castrated them, or he used another common barbaric method. Both cause unimaginable pain and suffering. He would have no way of doing either procedure with feral male cats though, since he couldn't handle them and wouldn't have access to sedating drugs. They would be released fertile too, along with the fertile females.

I asked him about the issue of relocating feral cats; ferals need to be detained for 3-5 weeks in a cage at the new location if there is any hope of them staying. He gave a vague, "we'll watch over 'em for you."

This guy was shrewd. He had nice feel-good answers about how he loved animals and only wanted to help. But anyone who would capture and then release fertile terrified feral cats in unfamiliar territory either doesn't understand animal welfare issues, or isn't concerned about them. This man was not an animal welfare advocate.

When I called the volunteer who had put me in touch with this trapper, he was dumbfounded that there was a fee, that the guy would dump the fertile cats, that he was performing cat neuters without benefit of anesthesia.

The lesson learned is perform due diligence. Never hand over vulnerable animals to someone who claims to be their friend without ensuring they really are.

In the end, we spayed/neutered about 30 cats from the area. All were owned or had committed caregivers. All got vaccinations, flea/tick treatments, ear tips, and topical dewormer before release. I photographed each feral cat we fixed from the farm supply company, and pasted the photo onto each cat's three-year rabies certificate. They kept those records in a file cabinet.

Certainly, what we did there helped. But my heart ached and tears spilled as I pulled out of that neighborhood for the last time. I could not look in the rear-view mirror. A myriad of animals in trouble, and we could not fix it. I grieve even now, recalling driving away and leaving behind animals in need.

That is though, animal welfare advocacy. You will not be able to help every animal who needs your assistance. It's why we must focus on getting these cats and dogs fixed. It is cheaper and it's easier than trying to rescue our way out of our country's animal overpopulation crisis. We did sterilize 30 cats, plus educated a business owner and some residents about spay/neuter surgery and standards of cat care. They are all the better for it.

And that trucker who alerted us to the cats? Over the years he's continued to send photos and updates about the cats we fixed near that truck terminal. Every time he passes through, we hear from him. Photos of shiny, bright-eyed, healthy looking cats with tipped ears make it worth it.

Listen more, talk less.

Talking instead of listening is another of my flaws. Listening first to the needs of those you are trying to help facilitates both of your goals. Telling pet owners what you're going to do and how you are going to do it won't be as effective or as efficient if you don't listen first to a pet owner's concerns. Listen first, talk later.

CHAPTER 28

Your Mission

AS THE DIRECTOR of the mighty but tiny nonprofit Homeless Animals Relief Project, I've tried to explain in this book how our grassroots group put more than 15,000 animals on the spay/neuter surgery table, all on an equally tiny budget, because I hope you'll take inspiration and roll up your sleeves. Our volunteers did this unpaid while working our regular jobs. If time isn't a gift you're able to give, we hope you will at least open your wallet. We want this book to raise money so we can offer more surgeries, so 100% of profits from this book are deposited into the animals' bank account. But most critical: We want you to spring into action. We need those who are younger and stronger and smarter and more skilled than us to advocate for animals. I've tried here to pass on the lessons I've learned, point out the pitfalls you may encounter, and expose my mistakes so you can visualize your path to helping animals too. Please carry on so the animals' gains will not be lost. The price of apathy is the agony of animals ignored.

Remember the animals in this book and in your life: Animals who endured, suffered, and loved humans just the same. Never forget the rest of the advocates: The veterinarians who toil to improve animal health daily, the owners desperate to find help for their pets, the organizations that fund the care we provide, the animal lovers who direct their estates to continue to advance animal welfare causes even after their deaths. Annie Lee Roberts, Muriel Slodden, and Dallas Pratt all benefited animals in their lifetimes and even after their passing, and we would never have fixed so many animals without their help. The advances against animal suffering that the Homeless Animals Relief Project have made would not have been possible without them or without the help and support of a myriad of people. We are all just shepherding animals home; sometimes the animals we lend a hand to are not our own.

Remember always that animal rescue is like holding a cup under a flowing tap and catching a little bit of the overflow while the rest flushes down the drain. Expensive and time consuming, rescue is an essential part of animal welfare, but it drains resources fast. Stopping the flow of unwanted and homeless animals through spay/neuter surgery must be your priority. We all know that which is not easily treated had better be prevented.

So, if you're concerned about the welfare of dogs and cats in America, please first focus on fixing animals. Rescue is required, as you gleaned from the stories. But using spay/neuter surgery to stop the flow of animals who will suffer must and should be your community's first priority. Opinions differ of course, but consider that most animal welfare organizations do not have unlimited resources. Which will yield the biggest improvement in our animals' welfare, reduction in their suffering, and aid in halting their overpopulation: An investment of $1000 curing a single dog of heartworms, or $1000 spent to have 20 dogs spayed and neutered? A gift of $10,000 to try to move 100 cats into homes, or $10,000 to fix 400 cats? Difficult decisions, yes. But spay/neuter surgery to reduce unwanted litters is a sustainable solution. It improves animal welfare immediately for the fixed animal, and benefits the whole community now and in the future.

You do have the ability to make a difference, and it's not all about money. Unless you're wealthy (and even if you are), your words and deeds are at least as important as money. Maybe these stories will spur the dream of enhancing animal welfare already germinating in your mind. If these stories prompt your ideas to ripen and blossom and grow, you'll ramp up the attacks on animal suffering. No more dying and suffering litters is a goal that really could be achieved in your lifetime. Please read and pass this book on, or better yet, buy another copy for a friend. And take the challenge. Don't delay. Do one thing today that will improve an animal's life. Fight the good fight for these creatures. Then let us know what you did.

CHAPTER 29

Hands-On

- Give local: Consider first supporting small grassroots charities in your area that provide spay/neuter surgery to pets living in low-income areas. Spay/neuter surgery halts the population overflow of suffering animals who need rescue and rehabilitation. We know that most of the animal overpopulation comes from impoverished families, so direct your resources to low-income areas first.

- Don't forget it's your dream, not always the pet owner's, to get the animal fixed; you may have to drive the pet to the vet appointment yourself. It's frustrating that you've offered a free pet fix to an owner who didn't show up for the appointment. But if you still want the pet sterilized, go get them and drive them yourself if necessary. Obviously, large or unfriendly dogs require the owner to get them into a crate and the car for you to transport. Do not get hurt trying to accomplish this goal. A bite wound can put you in the hospital and cost you your livelihood; a dog attack could cost you your life.

- Try to schedule a spay/neuter surgery date the same day an owner calls or agrees to the surgery; get them while they're interested. Calls about getting pets fixed should at the very least be returned the same day. Surgeries scheduled weeks or even months out increase the chance it won't get done. By then the owner has either lost interest or the pet.

- Ditch the hassles and excessive paperwork when offering spay/neuter surgery to low-income people. Complex registration and voucher protocols that require applicants to fill out lengthy forms or mail in copies of a driver's license, W-2s, and more will impede your goal to get pets fixed, not advance it. Paperwork places an additional burden on those who are unable to read or write at your level, and they'll promptly abandon or postpone the idea of getting their pet fixed. I received a brochure distributed by a humane organization that had a detailed, 14-step, outrageously complex process to just see if one would even qualify for a low-cost spay. Keep it simple. If you tour low-income neighborhoods to recruit pets for spay/neuter, you won't need owner proof of income when you witness their poverty first-hand.

- Recognize the appeal of vaccinations for owners who otherwise won't or can't get their pet to a vet. People who see no need to fix their pet may consent when offered a free 3-year rabies vaccination or routine vaccinations to go along with it.

- Consider bribes. I once gave a guy $20 to let our group cover the vet's spay surgery bill for his big mixed breed aging dog. Plus, I had to drive her to the appointment and drive her back home too. But when I pulled out that $20 bill, this guy instantly released his iron fist grip on the dog's collar, snatched the bill from me, pushed her towards me, and quit objecting to spay surgery. The sweet dog had no more puppies until she died years later. Her coat grew out shiny, bald spots filled in, she gained weight, and then spent her senescence encamped in the grass and basking in the sun. It was the best $20 I ever spent. I wish it wasn't like this. But if a bribe like pet food, vaccinations, or cash changes some minds and helps some animals, well, whatever works.

- Fix by five: Spread the word! Cats can come into heat at 14 weeks, and most will already be well into a pregnancy if that worn out old "wait until they are six months old" adage is followed. Learn more at FixbyFive.org. It's important.

- Promote and recruit for pet spay/neuter surgeries in low-income areas, working in teams, on pleasant Saturdays, between 10 am and 3 pm. Weekdays mean many will be away; Sundays are often religious or family days. We have the best results during those hours on Saturdays during mild, sunny weather. Good weather brings people and pets strolling through the neighborhood. It will be a fine time to recruit pets for your spay/neuter program, you'll make new friends, and you'll definitely have some interesting experiences. Look for groups of women to approach first; they seem to identify more with the issues of animal pregnancies and the resulting litters. Volunteers shouldn't travel alone, so two or more volunteers should team up for the touring. Put a cat trap, a cat crate, and a dog crate in your car. That enables a volunteer to take an animal right then if an owner agrees to spay/neuter but you don't believe they'll be willing or able to follow up with an appointment scheduled in the future.

- Use the term "animal birth control surgery" first when offering spay/neuter surgery to a pet owner. Multitudes of people don't know the definition of spay or neuter. You can also offer to "fix" the pet, but even that term may be understood.

- Wash the wound and seek medical care immediately if you are bitten by a cat or dog while trying to help them. Cat and dog bites can put you in the hospital for days; surgery and prolonged rehabilitation could be required if the bite is not treated immediately. We keep on hand the antibiotic recommended for cat bites by the United States Centers for Disease Control, and swallow the first dose if we are bitten, which is rare. Dogs more often inflict a crush injury, whereas cat bites can penetrate deeply and cause serious infections. Either way, see a healthcare provider right away.

- Know your local and state laws pertaining to animal welfare if you expect to intervene in a situation where you believe those animal welfare standards are not being met. Some states may only require that a pet owner provide food, water, and shelter, other states require more, such as necessary medical care, and a few locales might require sterilization of the pet. Local laws may also include leashing dogs and confining cats to indoors. You should know what is required in your community if you are to be an effective animal welfare advocate. Search the internet for your state laws, or visit your local public library. They'll find it for you.

- Know the limits of what you can do for an animal you believe is suffering. Contact a humane society, animal control officer, or dial 911 first before intervening. In a true emergency, where an animal is acutely suffering or dying— such as a dog locked in a hot car—your state or local laws may allow you to intervene immediately. Injured wildlife is typically covered by state and federal laws. Determine and learn the applicable laws in advance of need.

● Note that animal welfare advocates have been successfully criminally prosecuted for intervening in what they considered to be a suffering animal or animal cruelty situation, but the owners or a judge saw it differently. You won't be able to help any animals from a jail cell or while you're performing your community service hours and reporting to your parole officer. Again, look up these laws and know them in advance of need. Make a copy of the relevant section and keep it in your wallet, or take a screenshot of the current law and store it on your phone. Don't forget to review and update periodically to ensure you are current. An informed activist is a more effective activist.

● Find a vet who'll work with you to help animals. Then take all of your paying business to that vet. It's unfair to ask a compassionate, generous vet 20-miles away to offer discounted care to a stray dog when your own regular neighborhood vet has refused to do so. Yet you continue to patronize the neighborhood vet for your pets because that clinic is just so conveniently close. It probably wasn't convenient for the accommodating vet to help that stray when you asked, but he or she did. Put your money where your mouth is and drive the extra miles.

● Vaccinate feral cats against rabies when they are in your care for spay/neuter surgery. It's going to add about $3 to the cost of fixing each cat, but it promotes community health and makes you look like a good citizen. It's helpful to photograph each cat then paste that image onto the rabies form (usually available from your state, or your vaccine manufacturer). Give the record to the colony caregiver.

● Be an effective animal advocate if you're feeding stray cats or feral cats. Contact a feral cat program for help getting the cats spayed/neutered or talk to your vet; ensure cats' ears are tipped for identity. Avoid advertising the cats' presence or your kindness in feeding them; you'll likely stir up animosity and could endanger them. Always feed and water discreetly and never leave smelly, soggy, paper bowls or rotting cat food cans littering the area; that's guaranteed to generate complaints. Some municipalities have passed laws forbidding the feeding of homeless people. You can imagine the opposition there if you try to feed a homeless animal. If the feral cats you're discreetly feeding are discovered, work with nearby property owners and neighbors to negotiate a truce. The internet lists invaluable resources for feral cat caregivers, including Alley Cat Allies, Neighborhood Cats, and Feral Cat Coalition. Tap into their wisdom and experience.

- Know that adult feral cats are not likely to become friendly pets. Trying to transform an adult feral cat into a house pet will stress the cat and you; experts in feline welfare advise against it. Feral kittens often can be socialized up until about 8 weeks of age, so if you are hoping to place them, get started socializing them early. Kittens socialized before their fear imprinting period begins at about 6 weeks of age are most likely to make lifelong friendly pets. Handling kittens early and often gives them the greatest chance at becoming outgoing and social, which exponentially improves their chance of successful adoption. A cat who appears feral (hissing, spitting, striking, cowering with flattened ears, and spinning about in a crate or trap) may simply be a terrified pet. Once the cat has had a chance to settle over a few days, or even over a few weeks, you can better determine if she is truly feral or simply frightened. But it's difficult to make that determination on the spot. I've trapped homeless cats who acted wild and feral but a year later were following me about and wanting to be petted. However, that's not the same as becoming a socialized pet or lap cat, because they remained shy and unreceptive to other people.

- Consider whether feral cats have someone willing to take responsibility for their daily feeding, watering, and welfare checks before agreeing to trap–neuter–return a colony. Cats who are trapped, fixed, and then returned to areas where they are unwanted or have no advocate may not fare well. They likely will face food shortages, wild or feral dogs, wildlife, cars and traffic, and people who want them gone. Still, this is a debatable and complex ethical issue. There is no single answer that satisfies everyone; the issue draws opposing opinions and requires hard decisions. However, we no longer trap, fix, and return a feral or domesticated cat who has no responsible caregiver available. Other organizations will, saying that the cat has been living alone and can continue to do so, in better health even, if it has been sterilized and vaccinated. It's a decision you'll have to make. In our small community, we have so few volunteers and such limited resources that we direct our time and effort to helping feral cat colonies that have permission to remain, and someone willing to trap and transport and then monitor the colony. It's an oppressive but true fact that we have not enough people and money and vets to help all of the pets in our area. This is why fixing animals at an early age is so important.

● Accept the lamentable truth that not all animals will have the life we want for them. Sometimes bolstering up the life they have is the best that we can do. We can improve their lives with shelter, food/water deliveries, vaccinations, and sterilization surgery, but their lives may never rise to the level we dream of and desire for them. This is grievous and unfair, but it is reality.

● Don't reinvent the wheel. Look around for nonprofit spay/neuter clinics or groups to help before deciding to launch your own. If you do need to start a spay/neuter movement in your area, begin very small; line up a vet and get 2-5 pets fixed in a veterinary clinic. Then get 8-10 done. Then 12-15. Later shoot for 20-35. Grow from there. Do not draw up plans for a $3-million-dollar nonprofit spay/neuter surgery clinic and seek funding as your first priority. Work out the kinks and get your protocols in place first.

● Ask *your* pet's vet first for help if there is no local or nearby option for low cost or free spay/neuter surgeries. Could you bring 2–5 pets to his or her clinic for spay/neuter surgery one Saturday afternoon or Sunday, like a pop-up shop? This in-clinic spay/neuter surgery event is an ideal utilization of existing resources to help area pets. It eliminates the labor-intensive process of setting up and disassembling a separate spay/neuter surgery facility in another location. If your vet can't agree, move on until you find one who's open to trying the idea. You must expect to pay for this care; ask for donations. And never ever forget to say thank you.

● Decide all cats and dogs matter. A municipal shelter with no spay/neuter program and no affiliated veterinarian once called and asked if I could get veterinary students to come fix the shelter pets. "Probably," I replied. "They'll love the opportunity. Who's the vet you'll have supervising? The College of Veterinary Medicine will want that information and will have to approve your choice before it can be scheduled." "If I had a vet, I wouldn't need students," she replied. I explained these vet students were neither licensed nor fully experienced in surgical care of dogs and cats. Supervision by a licensed graduate vet to safely complete the surgeries would be required. She demurred on finding a veterinarian to supervise. Feeling that students could at least *try* to get the surgeries done, she said, "After all, these animals are going be euthanized anyway if they don't get adopted, and they probably won't, so what does it matter if they don't survive the surgery?" Most of us believe that all creatures, homeless or beloved, are entitled to veterinary care that meets basic professional standards. Make sure your care meets those standards too.

- Practice safe surgery. Have adequate emergency equipment wherever you are performing spay/neuter surgeries. This includes oxygen, a bag-valve-animal mask ventilating system and breathing tubes, and emergency drugs. Don't turn your back on anesthetized animals, their breathing could slow dangerously. They could vomit while anesthetized and the contents can become stuck in their throats, where it will occlude their airway. Have enough volunteers available to keep an eye on pets who've undergone anesthesia and surgery.

- Know that after 23 years and thousands of spay/neuter surgeries, our most common complication is postoperative bleeding after neuter in aged or adult male cats. They have well-developed testicles with a strong blood supply. Everything seems fine when they are discharged, but once they get home and start moving around, significant bleeding can begin. Check their bottoms carefully for bleeding before they are discharged; advise owners to call immediately if they see bleeding from a newly neutered male cat's surgical site. We've never had a kitten or juvenile male cat with a postoperative bleed; it's always been a hulking, beefy, adult male cat, so watch these big boys carefully. Because our owners often live so far away and in counties where there is no veterinary clinic for emergency follow-up, and because this bleeding can be severe, we started applying surgical clips in addition to the standard tie technique on all cat neuters. It's added insurance.

● Make volunteering fun: Get a laugh with a Cat Litterbox cake (recipe on internet). Let the volunteer who cleaned soiled crates wear a lovely plastic tiara for the day; give departing volunteers cheap party favors like a toy for their pet, a gift card for a deli sandwich, or even a t-shirt, etc. And don't forget to say thank you as they walk out the door.

● Move pregnant animals and those in heat to the top of the spay/neuter surgery list. Get them to a veterinarian fast for examination. In our area we have high euthanasia rates of cats and kittens in shelters. We also have no area shelters or rescues currently accepting cats, so unwanted cats/kittens have no place to go. Is it reasonable to allow more kittens or puppies to be born when we are killing the ones who are already here? No, not under our circumstances. You may find conditions different in your community. But it's important to realize that spay surgery can be safely and humanely performed during pregnancy.

● Review the free materials available on the internet about starting or setting up a spay/neuter surgery clinic, if this is the path you choose. There's a bounty of data on best practices, forms, suggestions, and helpful videos.

● Attend animal welfare conferences that focus on spay/neuter advocacy once you decide you need to start a program in your area, or if you want to network with other advocates. You'll learn volumes and meet face to face with those who can move you forward.

● Consider all facets before inviting volunteers under the age of 18; we do not accept minors because of liability issues when dealing with animals. Even when accompanied by a parent, we've had issues with reliability and usefulness. We've found it's better to curate a group of experienced, responsible adults from the community to form a pool of volunteers from which you can draw. Youth interested in animal welfare should of course be encouraged, but they may be best served in programs designed for their participation.

- Understand that each new kitten or pup born may force the euthanasia of an animal already in the shelter awaiting a home. Owners will proudly proclaim "we always find them good homes" when speaking of their pet's litters, but every "good" home taken up by their pet's offspring means a door slammed shut to a shelter animal, followed by the opening of the door to the euthanasia room. Reiterate this to those who let their pet breed, whether for the children's entertainment or because of their own inertia. On the other side is the adoption of a shelter dog or cat—you save two animals: The first is the one you adopted, the second is the one who moved from death row into that now empty cage in the adoption area.

- Avoid giving dogs and cats away free, because that is about what they will be worth to some adopters. Request a reasonable adoption fee that helps get the pet into a responsible non-impulse home, but isn't so high that they'll decide to take a giveaway pet instead. Explain that a spayed kitten with a $50 adoption fee is cheaper than a free one, because she's already been vetted and fixed. Always follow-up on adoptions to ensure all is going well or to re-evaluate the placement.

- Understand a miserably common cycle of homelessness in cats: Family adopts cute kitten because kids begged for a kitten. Kids play with kitten for a week or so, then she's pushed out the door because she's started scratching the furniture and the kids have lost interest anyway. Kids forget to feed kitten, who goes to neighbor's house and eats their cat's food. Neighbor won't get this kitten spayed because this is not her cat, she won't pay to fix someone else's cat, and she's concerned she'd be in trouble if she did take a cat that isn't hers to surgery. The adopters refuse to spend money on the cat because she is always at the neighbor's house; they never see her anymore, and they've lost interest anyway. So, cat has litter, kittens hide under the shed, aren't socialized, and all turn feral. Cycle repeats. Always spay or neuter kittens before placement.

- Don't place any pet for adoption who hasn't been fixed. Never. Ever. It's unethical to promote yourself as an animal welfare advocate, preach the vital role of spay/neuter surgery, but then admit you couldn't afford to get the pet fixed and sure hope the adopter can. Our organization receives calls from groups who acknowledge they've spent their veterinary care budget on a rescue animal's medical needs, now have zero dollars for essential spay/neuter surgery, and they would like us to take on that responsibility for them. Ethical, legitimate rescues fix pets before adoption. Work with a vet who'll give you a reasonable price, and build that into your adoption fee. You may have an adopter you trust to get the animal fixed, but things can and will happen to prevent that sure thing; I speak from bitter experience. And forget writing future spay/neuter surgery requirements into an adoption contract. Any cat who's old enough to be placed in a home is old enough to be fixed. Kittens should not be taken from their mothers before 8 weeks of age, and they can be safely fixed at that time.

- Investigate carefully before handing over multiple pets to one person, especially someone who isn't interested in seeing them first and doesn't care if they are fixed. Once, we had arranged the spay/neuter surgery of 15 barn kittens. The day before the surgeries, I called the owner to remind her. "I gave them away," she said. "This guy said he wanted them all and he took them." She was pleased; you and I are sickened. Free cats, kittens, and small dogs are vulnerable to nefarious people with sinister and evil purposes. Don't give pets away free.

- Be wary of the catchphrase "no kill" if you decide to donate to rescue groups. There is no standard for the use of this jazzy buzzword in animal welfare. It sucks in cash like a casino, so you could be giving money to organizations that advertise "no kill" but do. Sometimes the fine print claims they only euthanize "unadoptable" animals, but your definition of what constitutes unadoptable could differ from theirs. You could also be donating to organizations that will cage and confine or warehouse dogs and cats with little socialization, comfort, exercise, or interaction for the rest of their lives in order to maintain that "no kill" status. If a "no kill" facility is full, the group might place pets without adopter evaluation, support, or follow-up. Pets sometimes will even be offered free in order to reduce the number in the organization's care. Small dogs and kittens are especially vulnerable to cruel endings; use due diligence. If an organization claims extraordinarily high adoption rates, give thanks but investigate further before you donate.

- Do your research on any animal rescue organization before donating. Many animal welfare organizations operate as 501(c)3 tax exempt public charities under federal laws. You can ask an organization for a copy of their Form 990, Return of Organization Exempt from Income Tax; they are required to provide it. This will show you how they spend donations received. Go to irs.gov, then Charities & Nonprofits, then search for the charity you are considering supporting. If they are registered as a nonprofit you can view online the tax forms they've submitted. Small organizations with budgets less than $50,000/year typically file "postcard" returns, thus you will not receive detailed information on very small groups.

- Remember that offering spay/neuter surgery is your proactive step to reduce the need for rescue, placement, and sheltering of unwanted animals. You work hard for your money; make it work hard for our animals. This is important.

- Visit the rescue organization yourself to see the animals you'll be helping, if you decide to support rescue operations. Won't let you visit? Won't let you in certain areas? Don't give money.

- Volunteer at spay/neuter surgery clinics too, not just rescues. Animal rescue is filled with captivating, heartwarming, and at times horrifying tales; it is hands-on with animals in need. So is spay/neuter surgery, your foundational concept in promoting pet welfare. These clinics need your help too.

- Don't give money to rescues who do not spay or neuter pets before adoption. It's unfair to the pet being placed and it perpetuates the overpopulation that necessitates rescue, becoming a perverse self-fulfilling cycle. One public shelter near us offered a dog in the local newspaper for adoption, stating she was friendly and loving but acknowledging she had been adopted and then returned twice. The reason? "She keeps having puppies."

- Offer your skills to a spay/neuter advocacy nonprofit group. Maybe you don't want to go toe-to-toe with pet owners or try to recruit vets. Maybe you don't want to monitor surgical patients or clean cages, or your circumstances prevent that. Everyone has a talent the animals need and can use. If you're an attorney, offer your legal expertise to those working the front lines, or to small grass roots efforts. If you're an accountant, help with the group's taxes or 501(c)3 application. If you're a truck driver, offer to transport animals. If you're a landscaper, mow a yard to free up a volunteer to drive a pet to spay/neuter surgery, or help keep the spay/neuter clinic lawn tidy and appealing. If you're a plumber, repair that leaky pipe in the surgery clinic at no charge. If you're a stay-at-home mom, maybe you could answer the calls requesting spay/neuter care for the group; a dedicated cell phone makes this easy. One of our pet owners, a housecleaner, dropped off her three cats for spay/neuter surgery in the morning. That afternoon when she returned, she brought her bucket, mops, broom, rubber gloves, bags, and rags with her to help us clean up. The animals need everyone's skills.

• Donate your time and money to your area nonprofit spay/neuter surgery clinics. America has huge multimillion-dollar national animal welfare charities doing good work. But funds donated to national organizations don't always trickle down to small grassroots efforts, and when they do, those grant recipients may feel like they're tap dancing on a razor blade. I regret accepting a $1000 grant from a national animal welfare group. Along with their grant came pages of demands, including their logo front and center and exact specified pixel size (BIG!) on our webpage, and press releases I was required to send about their involvement. Nearly unlimited reports and redundant documentation was expected in return for the money. Then the paperwork would be returned for re-do; a submitted invoice proved the vet's bill had been paid, but it was rejected because it didn't indicate what *tender* (Cash? Check? Credit card?) was presented as payment. Onerous paperwork reduces our ability to help the animals the grant was intended for, and it freezes weary boots to the ground. I never approached them again. Think small and think local when you give.

• Look for the 501(c)3 or other acceptable charity designation before you give. 501(c)3 charities have applied for and been granted nonprofit charity status by the federal government. Once the designation is awarded, donors' gifts are tax deductible to the extent allowed by law, and the designation also bestows some credibility. If you must launch your own mission to fix pets or an animal welfare group, you'll need the designation if you do decide to apply for grant funds. Don't reinvent the wheel though. Is there is an organization in your area offering spay/neuter surgeries for pets living with the poor? Consider throwing your support to them rather than starting another group.

- Ignore people who've helped you help animals, if you want to guarantee they won't help again. Better idea: Buy a stack of blank adhesive postcards, affix it to a photo of a pet that was altered with their donation, and mail it with a heartfelt thank you message. Later get some customized thank you cards printed.

- Mail "thanks for getting your pet fixed" postcards to each person whose pet you fix, and ask them to pass that card on to others. You can design these online. The purpose in sending a card is to reinforce the desired behavior (getting their pet fixed) and to encourage them to discuss it with friends, passing the card on to them. This helps us achieve our goal of getting pets fixed.

- Pace yourself. Don't let robust enthusiasm for animal welfare blind you to the reality of burnout or cause you to ignore your own welfare. Balance helping other people's animals with enjoying your own. If you ignore your family, they might go away.

- Send impact reports to those who make larger contributions; include photos of the pets and people they helped. This is a letter detailing how their gift was spent and how many animals benefited. Everyone who gives money to animal welfare loves to look into the eyes of animals they've helped; this increases the chance they'll give again.

- Paint animal welfare as a pest control issue first when addressing community leaders; leave the compassionate animal care lecture for later. Sadly, many politicians and administrators are more concerned about cash and budgets than what's ethical or who's suffering. Explain how sterilization of pets reduces shelter intakes, and fixing and vaccinating feral cats benefits the community. Document how intact dogs are the ones most often involved in aggression and attacks, and prove that catch and kill doesn't work. (Search the internet to get the stats you'll need). Leaders are more likely to listen to your pitch if you offer them a way to save money while looking good. Spay/neuter surgery saves money and makes them look good. Most communities spend well over $100 per cat or dog to catch, process intake, house/feed for a mandatory period, euthanize, then dispose of the remains. Spay/neuter surgery costs less, before we even get to the kindness and decency part.

- Never ever detach from the beauty, the mystery, the love of the animals you are helping. Stay with it, remember it, feel it. We are all kin and we share that kinship. All of creation is traveling home together. We are on the same road. We are walking side by side. Listen to those animals sharing the path with you, feast on their beauty. Touch and feel and know these precious living creatures. You will receive encouragement, love, strength for your journey, and sweet companionship.

- Finally, consider supporting our charity. I want to inspire you to help animals, but my second purpose in writing this book is to raise funds to help more animals here in rural Mississippi. *One hundred percent of the profits from this book will go to the animals we help.* You can donate online at www.homelessanimalsreliefproject.org, or mail a check to HARP, P. O. Box 371, Senatobia, MS 38668. When you mail a check, the animals get all of your gift without the fees that must be paid to collect online donations.